CANADA

The Beautiful Land

CLB 1320
© 1985 Illustrations and text: Colour Library Books Ltd.,
    Guildford, Surrey, England.
Illustrations on pages 51, 84, 85, 86, 87, 193. 197, 200, 201,
378, 379, 380, 381, 383, 384, 385, 386, 387, 388, 389, 390, 391,
392, 393, 394, 395, 396, 397, 398, 399, 400 copyright © Parks Canada.
Text filmsetting by Acesetters Ltd., Richmond, Surrey, England.
Printed and bound in Barcelona, Spain.
All rights reserved.
ISBN 0 86283 388 4
Dep. Leg. B.28.280-85

CANADA
The Beautiful Land

Text by
Bill Harris

B. Mitchell

CONTENTS

If you stop by the general store in Edmundston, New Brunswick, they'll sell you just about anything you need. But if you want a candy bar, you'll have to buy that in the United States. No one will ask you to leave the store, though. They'll just ask you to step around to the candy counter. And when you do, you'll be stepping across the international boundary that separates the second-largest country in the world from her smaller neighbor to the south.

It's a casual boundary for most of its 3,986 miles, and in places like Edmunston, folk hardly even notice it's there. In one house, the line runs right through the middle of the kitchen and kids raiding the cookie jar risk an international incident every time they reach for another piece of shortbread. In some places along the border, mailmen from the United States include Canadian farmers in their daily rounds just because it's easier for everybody that way.

If someone from British Columbia tells you they've just bought a house in the country, you might well ask "what country?" because vacation homes in the state of Washington are very popular among people from Vancouver. Young people from Maine go to Quebec, where the legal drinking age is lower, for their nights on the town. And Detroit factory workers looking for a great Italian meal often head south (yes, south!) across the border to Windsor, Ontario.

All that international travel is second nature to Americans and Canadians, many of whom have solid roots on the opposite side of the border from the one that's home to them now. The largest single group of people who have migrated to Canada in the last 150 years came from the British Isles, but Yankees from south of the border are a very close second. In fact, back and forth migration by Canadians and Americans has totalled more than six million people, one of the greatest population movements in history.

It has an effect on family life, too. It's not unusual at all for brothers and sisters to have different nationalities yet live under the same roof. Nor is it unusual for a Canadian man to work in the United States while his wife goes to work in Canada and for both of them to spend a Saturday afternoon in an American shopping center where their Canadian money is accepted at the same rate as the higher-valued Yankee dollar.

Some 70 million people cross the U.S./Canadian border every year virtually unchallenged. But that's not to say the border isn't a very real thing. Back in the early 1950s they built an airport in Pinecreek, Minnesota to serve the growing number of private planes carrying hunters, fishermen and businessmen into Canada. It was a great idea. It put Pinecreek on the map and gave some relief to the airports at Minneapolis and Winnipeg by eliminating the necessity of stopping there to clear customs.

Except for gopher holes in the runway, things went smoothly for twenty years. Oh, the Canadian customs officers complained a lot about having to traipse across the border from Piney, Manitoba, Pinecreek's sister city, every time a plane passed through, but they didn't really mind. The real trouble came when private planes started getting bigger but the airport didn't.

The solution was obvious: lengthen the runway. But that was easier said than done. The runway stopped right smack on the border, which meant that extending it northward would take it into Canada. Lengthening it to the south would mean closing an important road, so the people of Piney and Pinecreek got together and drafted an agreement to let the airport cross into Canada.

Officials in Ottawa didn't like the agreement and a lot of time was lost getting it just right. Down in Washington it was discovered that approval required an act of Congress and once that was accomplished, the Canadian Government ruled that a little town like Piney had no business entering into agreements with foreign governments. Another new law was needed. The whole process took seven years, but finally the job was done and the world had its first "binational" airport. It's still just a grassy strip and traffic is still light, but it sits there as a reminder that this border, usually touted as the longest and oldest undefended border in the world, is made up, in some places at least, of the same red tape as any other.

Most American schoolchildren have learned about the battle of Lake Erie and the boast of Oliver Hazard Perry that he had met the enemy and stood up to them. It's the stuff of patriotism. What seems to have been lost since he met the enemy in 1813 is that he had the enemy fleet hugely outnumbered and that the "enemy" was Canada. The fight was essentially a war between the United States and its giant neighbor to the north.

In spite of the fact that no less a person than Thomas Jefferson had said, "The acquisition of Canada will be a mere matter of marching...," and a high official in the Madison administration had boasted, "We can take the Canadas without soldiers," the Canadians made a better showing for themselves on the battlefield than their attackers and the treaty that ended the war did little more than reestablish the original border; the border they call peaceful today.

The 1812 war wasn't the first time, nor the last, that Americans stormed into Canada with fire in their eyes and guns in their hands. It happened in 1775, even before the American Declaration of Independence had been signed, when Ethan Allen led a force of "patriots" in an attack on Ticonderoga and Crown Point at the foot of Lake Champlain. Moving right along, they took Montreal just as winter was setting in, and then, joined by a larger force headed by Benedict Arnold, they kept Quebec City under siege until spring. Finally, on a fine day in May, 1776, they decided to turn around and go home. The British at Quebec, who by then had been reinforced by way of the St. Lawrence River, didn't bother to follow them, probably because there still wasn't a formal state of war between Britain and her American colonies. To the defenders,

Quebec was just another colony like Virginia and Massachusetts. In fact, the other colonies seemed to feel the same way. When the first Continental Congress convened in 1774, the colony of Quebec was invited to send delegates. If they hadn't refused, the American flag might have 14 stripes today, and the map of North America might look a bit different, too.

The American Founding Fathers overlooked Nova Scotia when they were sending out invitations, even though thousands of New Englanders who had settled there were very much in favor of independence from the Mother Country. By the time the Americans tried to "liberate" that colony, the British Navy turned them away.

The next obvious step was for the British to use Canada as a base of operations for their war against the southern colonies. The attack that followed, led by "Gentleman Johnny" Burgoyne, wound up in a British defeat at Saratoga that turned the way around for the Americans and just about took Canada out of it altogether. In the treaty that ended the whole thing, Britain retained control of Quebec, Nova Scotia, Newfoundland and the huge territory to the north called "Rupert's Land," named for Prince Rupert, the cousin of King Charles II who had been given a charter to all the land around Hudson's Bay for the purpose of fishing, trapping, mining, controlling a water route to China, if any, or whatever else the prince might like to do.

The treaty also established the boundary between Canada and the United States. It would be a long time in the future before anyone could call it "peaceful."

While hotheads in Boston and Philadelphia were shouting for independence, a lot of their neighbors got a different kind of message: "get out of town." In the 13 lower colonies, these people who didn't want independence were called "Tories," and were generally considered antisocial. Up north, they were called "Loyalists," and were very welcome in local society.

There were even more Americans who migrated north not because of their politics, but because of a lack of them. All they wanted was to find the promise of "rugged individualism" that had lured them to America in the first place. They could find it in Canada, and it didn't matter a bit to them that they were under the control of some king across the ocean.

Neither group was too enamored with the new country to the south. The Tories had been forced out, usually leaving their possessions behind them. At the end of their revolution, the Americans had promised to restore any property the Tories had lost, but it was a promise that was never kept and that left a lot of Canadians resentful of Americans to say the least.

On their side of the border, a lot of Americans returned the resentment. Almost as soon as they got their independence, they began expanding their country to the west. Of course, there were already some people there: the Indians. North of the Great Lakes, people were interested in moving west, too, but in the main they were fur trappers and traders and the Indians knew it was good business to let them come. But the people who were crossing the Appalachians into Ohio and Indiana were settlers and farmers and, to the Red Man, that was bad business.

The Indians responded by attacking farms and settlements, aided, the American settlers were convinced, by their neighbors in Canada. The Americans were also still licking the wounds of the recent war, and most didn't like the idea of having a British colony at their doorstep. It had to come to a head sooner or later, and it did when the U.S. declared war on Great Britain in 1812.

The next invasion across the border, about 25 years later, came from the Canadian side. As a British colony, Canada was divided into two distinct entities, Upper Canada and Lower Canada. The terms were geographical only. In reality, the upper half was extremely low on the British list of priorities. Added to that, as an inland territory, the colonists to the north and west were dependent on their more privileged neighbors in Montreal for access to the ocean and the rest of the world. A lot of Americans heading west wound up in Upper Canada, whose boundaries were roughly similar to the Province of Ontario today. A lot of new immigrants from Britain wound up there, too, including huge numbers from Scotland and Ireland. It was a volatile mix that finally exploded in 1837, when a Scottish newspaperman named William Mackenzie issued a declaration of independence for Upper Canada and marched on "the industrial overlords" in Toronto. It took the overlords about 15 minutes to put down the revolt and Mackenzie slipped across the border into the United States, disguised as a little old lady.

He came back to Canada with a better-organized band of rebels and managed to capture a little spit of land in the Niagara River, which he established as "The Republic of Canada." American sympathizers kept him supplied from their side of the river with daily trips in a steamboat called the *Caroline*. In retaliation, Canadian militiamen boarded the boat in a surprise attack and, after having put the crew ashore, towed her out to the middle of the river where they set her afire and cut her adrift in the general direction of Niagara Falls. The ship broke up in the rapids before going over, but rumors on the American side had it that the burning ship had plunged over the falls with her full crew piteously crying for help. The rumors were not true, of course, but they made for a lot of American hostility toward Canada. For once the American Government kept cool, and when Mackenzie abandoned his little country for the safety of the American side, he was arrested for violating neutrality laws and spent nearly a year in jail.

That didn't stop the rumors, though, and all over the United States men banded together to avenge the *Caroline*, and not incidentally, to escape the depression in their country and go to Canada, where Mackenzie had offered free land to able bodied men who helped him in his fight.

About a thousand of them crossed the St. Lawrence River in 1838 and took control of a windmill at Precott, Ontario. They held it for nearly a week, but finally were routed. The leaders were hanged and many others were sent to the British equivalent of Devil's Island.

A lot of opportunists conducted similar, if smaller, raids until the whole business was settled by treaty in 1842. But if things were quieted in the East, there was a whole new problem the two countries would have to face: The Wild West.

From the earliest times, one of the prime reasons for exploring the North American continent had been to find a water route across it to get at the riches of the East. In 1776, the British decided to try looking from the other side of the continent and dispatched their ace explorer, Captain James Cook, to sail up the Pacific coast of North America to see if he could find a passage heading east toward the Atlantic. It took him more than a year, but he finally put ashore on Vancouver Island which, according to an old Russian map he had, was just a hop, skip and a jump from Alaska. The Russian map-maker was convinced Alaska was a big island. His map showed a wide river running from there up to the polar ocean, which the Russian implied was navigable. Cook spent close to six months looking for the river, but all he found was the Bering Strait. But even in late August it was too full of ice for his ships to get through.

At that point, Cook decided it was time he looked for a warmer place to explore and set sail for Hawaii, where the natives abruptly ended his career. His logs and charts survived, though, and greatly intensified the search for the North American transverse, which everyone was convinced must be across Canada.

The rush was on among explorers who wanted to be first

to see it. One of them drew a map, based as much on fancy as fact, that showed a connecting system of rivers and lakes. From what Indians had told him and what he had seen for himself, he was sure that the Pacific Ocean was not only easily reached by water, but that the trip was surprisingly short. When he saw that fanciful map, a young Scot named Alexander Mackenzie decided to follow it.

He found a river flowing out of Great Slave Lake and followed it west. According to the map, the Rocky Mountains didn't go that far north and the ocean wasn't far beyond. But about 300 miles downstream, he discovered the map was wrong on at least one count: the Rockies were there, even more forbidding than they were in the South. Worse, the river, which had been flowing west, was turning around on them and heading north. He kept going anyway and didn't give up until he reached the end, a delta network of confusing little islands. He put ashore on one of the islands to have a look around, but all he could see ahead was tightly-packed ice. With that, he named the waterway "River of Disappointment" and turned around for the long trip back against the current.

What he discovered, of course, was the biggest river in Canada, which long since has been named for him. And except for the disappointment of thinking he had proven for all time that there was no such thing as a Northwest Passage, the trip was a huge success. Because of it, the British colonies in Canada expanded by more territory than all of Europe.

Mackenzie wasn't completely convinced that there was no Northwest Passage. The fault, he was sure, was in his lack of understanding of navigation. To remedy that, he took a year off from his fur trading business and went to college in London. When he got back, he set off on a second expedition, partly on foot this time, to find a practical way to get across the continent. It was far from easy, but his company covered 1200 miles in 74 days and finally Mackenzie left some grafitti on a rock overlooking the Pacific Ocean telling the world: "Alexander Mackenzie, from Canada by land, the 22nd of July, 1793." They were the first men to cross the continent, and a little more than a month later they had crossed it again on the return trip. The expedition opened the Pacific Northwest to the fur trade, which in turn made Mackenzie a wealthy man, and that, in turn, gave him enough leisure time to write a book about his adventures in what he called "this magnificent theater of nature." The book was an instant hit. King George III of England was so impressed he conferred a knighthood on the explorer. Napoleon Bonaparte used it as the basis for a never-tried plan to attack Canada and take it away from the English. But the biggest stir of all was caused in Washington when the American president, Thomas Jefferson, read the book and American-Canadian relations took another nasty turn.

Jefferson, the third American president, had paid $15,000,000 to Napoleon Bonaparte for a French-American colony called Louisiana, which had been French territory since the French explorer LaSalle had gone down the Mississippi River to expand "New France," as they called Canada in 1681, all the way down to the Gulf of Mexico. The territory included in the deal extended north along the river to Lake Superior and west as far as the Rocky Mountains. It was a complicated transaction, to be sure, and untangling some secret deals the French had made with the Spanish took more than 15 years. In that time an American explorer, Captain Robert Gray, had discovered the Columbia River and a Canadian, David Thompson, had traced it to its source in an expedition every bit as harrowing as Mackenzie's cross-country jaunt.

John Jacob Astor, a New Yorker with a flair for making money, had sent a ship around Cape Horn to the mouth of the Columbia and established a trading post there which he modestly called "Astoria." Captain George Vancouver, a veteran of Cook's expedition, had explored and mapped the Northwest coast and, of course, claimed it for Great Britain. The Russians, meanwhile, had stepped over into Alaska and their search for sea otter skins, for which the Chinese seemed willing to pay any price, had taken them south into territory the British and the Americans both coveted. At the same time, the Spanish, who had settled California, claimed some of the same territory. The situation, quite simply, was a mess.

When Jefferson heard about Mackenzie's adventures, he decided it was time for the United States to get into the act with an expedition of its own. He had been talking about it for years with his private secretary, Captain Meriwether Lewis, who recruited his friend William Clark to help him actually put the expedition together. The trip was billed as an effort to have a look at the territory Jefferson had bought from France. But while they were at it, they said, they might just as well push all the way to the Pacific to look in on the Astor colony.

The round trip took two years and four months, a good bit longer than Mackenzie's 74 days. They spent more of their time making maps and writing descriptions, though, and the picture they painted made the Pacific Northwest seem like a Garden of Eden to Americans back East. The Lewis and Clark expedition was so well-publicized, in fact, most Americans even today think it was the first to cross the North American continent, in spite of the fact that Mackenzie had beaten them to it by nearly a dozen years.

But Americans have always responded enthusiastically to good public relations, and thousands responded in the early 19th century by heading west over Lewis and Clark's Oregon Trail. In Canada, most of the migrants were trappers and other hardy souls willing to put up with a couple of years of hardship for a life of wealth and ease. The Americans were farmers looking for better land to turn into farms. The Oregon Trail was no superhighway, but the trails across Canada were much more forbidding and hostile, and Canadians looking for a permanent new life in the West generally went south first and threw in their lot with the Americans.

The result was that of the four countries with a claim on the Pacific Coast, the Americans had an important edge: people. It's one thing to plant a flag or to paint your name on a rock, but quite another to send in settlers.

Even more Americans went west when gold was discovered in California in 1849. It would be ten more years before it was discovered on the Fraser River in Canada and by then there were more Americans within striking distance of the source than there were Canadians.

The Colony of British Columbia was very much in danger of becoming a "little California" in the process and the old colony on Vancouver Island felt it had plenty to worry about, too. The London Government combined them into one colony in the interest of strength and crossed its fingers that the Washington Government would honor its treaty establishing the U.S./Canadian border along the 49th parallel. Washington, meanwhile, was talking about another big real estate deal. This time they proposed to buy Alaska from the Russians. It was only natural for the Canadian colonists to feel that they were being surrounded. It didn't help a bit when James Polk ran for president in the United States with a slogan that said "54-40 or fight!," implying that the Oregon border should be extended north to Alaska and if the British objected there would be a war.

When he actually was elected, he went to war with Mexico instead and added California and most of the Southwest to his country. That seemed enough for him because he accepted the 49th parallel as the Canadian border and even agreed (without a fight) to let the British keep all of Vancouver Island.

During those years, Canada was planning for its own future. In 1841, Upper and Lower Canada were united and for the first time Canadians were beginning to think of something more than just surviving. The French Canadians in the East still felt like a nation apart, but for all

practical purposes, the union created a British presence in North America that no one in the world could ignore.

The British presence also meant British money, and millions of pounds were spent to improve the canal system along the St. Lawrence River as well as to build roads and improve harbors in order to make Canada self-sufficient as a trading partner in the British Empire. Most important, though, was the money that built the transcontinental railroads that connected, if not united, the Maritime Provinces in the East with the rich Pacific Northwest.

It was a boom time for Canada. But then the old grudge between Mother England and her offspring in the United States came back to haunt the Canadians one more time.

It happened when the United States declared war on itself over the issue of slavery in 1861. Canadians in general were against slavery and their sympathies were with the North in the American Civil War. But in England, the general policy was to support the Confederacy and England was more important to the future of Canada than the United States was. In the years before the war, escaped slaves had been transported across the border into Canada to get them out of harm's way. When the war made a draft necessary, draft dodgers by the thousands followed them. Rich Southern planters sent their wives and children into Canada, too, giving Canada a rather odd mixed-bag of Americans to deal with.

The Confederacy sent hundreds of special agents to Toronto and Montreal to take advantage of British sympathy and to use Canada as a base for raids across the border. It was actually tried only once, when a band of Southerners set out from Montreal to attack the town of St. Albans, Vermont. They made the mistake of financing their raid with the proceeds of the robbery of a Canadian bank and so never made it further than the border.

They had also planned to capture a Union steamer on the Great Lakes, but one of the conspirators got drunk one night and bragged a little too much, giving the whole plot away. Their most imaginative plan was to move from Canada into Chicago disguised as, of all things, delegates to the Democratic National Convention. That one didn't work, either.

Canadian patience held the day, but their real problems began after the war was over. Rebel raiders working out of Canada had destroyed some Union shipping and in its fury against England for siding with the Confederates, the American Congress proposed that, as a war reparation, the Grand Army of the Republic should now march north and take all of Canada.

Not many took the idea seriously, but the idea caught fire with a group of Irishmen bound together in a society called the Fenian Brotherhood. They were passionate about the idea of freeing Ireland from British rule, and just as passionate in their hatred of anything British. They called for an invasion on St. Patrick's Day in 1866, but they couldn't get their act together before June, when about 2000 of them crossed the border into Ontario. They managed to capture Fort Erie on the Niagara River, but soon decided to go home to the American side, where they were picked up by American authorities. About half of them were arrested and then released. Four years later they attacked again and, though virtually unopposed, retreated home again after a short spree of burning and looting. They were arrested again and never tried attacking Canada after that.

Their hostility convinced both Canadian and British officials that it was time they did something about uniting these colonies into a country. They had been talking about getting together for more than one hundred years, but it wasn't until 1867 that all the pieces fell into place when the British Parliament created a union of four provinces – Ontario, Quebec, Nova Scotia, and New Brunswick. It was a new Canada, free and independent, with its own government and its own destiny.

In the same year Canadians agreed to confederation, the United States concluded its deal with Russia to buy Alaska. Thirty years later, a gold rush in the Klondike caused the next and, for all practical purposes, last confrontation between the two neighboring countries. Both the United States and Canada had never stopped arguing about the Oregon border, but nothing serious came of any of it, and there weren't enough people along the Alaska border to cause any serious argument.

But the gold rush brought in plenty of people and a lot of the prospectors from Alaska brought their own equipment with them. The Canadians said they should pay an import duty, but to collect the tax they had to set up customs stations along the border. The problem was that nobody knew exactly where the border was. An international commission was set up, of course, but Teddy Roosevelt, who was the American president at the time, covered his bets by sending troops into Alaska to protect the American citizens there. The British got the message and voted with the Americans against what the Canadians felt were their best interests. The Canadians found a message there, too, and decided it was time to start taking charge of their own foreign affairs and defense. It took them a while to accomplish it. Finally, after having lost 60,000 of its young men in World War I, a war most French Canadians and people living in rural areas considered none of their business, their campaign paid off with the Statute of Westminster, which in 1931 finally made it official that Great Britain and her Dominions had become "autonomous communities within the British Empire, equal in status, in no way subordinate to one another in any aspect of their domestic or external affairs, though united by a common allegiance to the Crown, and freely associated as members of the British Commonwealth of Nations."

One thing the Statute of Westminster didn't do for Canada was give her the power to amend the British North America Act of 1867. Originally the Act was intended to give Canada a strong central government, but the Provinces were never really willing to give away their power and over the years interpretations of constitutional law have generally agreed with that philosophy, each time taking away a little more power from the government in Ottawa.

A great many Canadians considered the constitution illegal anyway because it was drafted by the British. Others were fond of pointing out that the world had changed a whole lot since 1867 and it was about time some of these laws were changed, too.

The debate raged for years, and it was obviously only a matter of time before a purely Canadian constitution would be drafted and turned into the law of the land. One force that pushed hard in that direction was the result of a clause in the 1867 document known as Article 133. "Either the English or the French language may be used by any person in the debates of the Houses of Parliament of Canada," it said. And it went on to add, "...and of the Houses of the legislature of Quebec." The article applied to Manitoba as well, but not officially to the other Canadian Provinces.

The Canadian Provinces have never really been united, but not many Canadians took the idea of complete separateness seriously until 1967, when Canada celebrated its hundredth anniversary as a nation with a World's Fair in Montreal. The show was a huge success and showed the world that Canada was indeed a going concern. But one of the guests, Charles de Gaulle of France, made a speech that gave new life to the cause of the Separatists. Quebec ought to be free and independent, he said, and thousands cheered.

The Quebecois formed their own political party and less than 10 years later they elected their own premier, who made French the only official language in the province. But in the meantime, the Federal Government was headed by

12

another French Canadian, Pierre Trudeau, whose policy was to help the French-speaking people, but not at the expense of the country as a whole.

Today, after years of wrangling and debate, Canada has her Constitution and sovereignty, finally agreed on in November 1981 and handed over by the British Monarch in April of 1982.

Canada grew by evolution rather than revolution. Canadians have never fought a war for survival that could produce the national heroes and national myths that inspire patriotism and a common identity. But they usually will agree to one important thing that makes all Canadians proud: the fact that they're not Americans.

Of course it's inevitable that Canadians compare themselves and their institutions to their neighbors in the United States, but the more they do, the more they swell with pride in the fact that they are Canadians and not like Americans at all.

Outsiders sometimes see that as a disadvantage. The British poet Rupert Brooke wrote that "Canada is a live country; live, but not like the States, kicking." A Canadian historian pointed out that because the land itself is so hostile, the climate so bleak, the early pioneers who settled the country were so often faced by defeat that they learned to accept it. Americans, on the other hand, he said "...can't conceive of losing unless there's a conspiracy somewhere. Canadians, constrained by climate, distance and history, see no reason to expect victory."

That's not to say Canadians are held back by a defeatist attitude. Far from it. But many, especially in the West, are content to put their faith in themselves and not depend on any institutions to help them or to share in their successes.

Less than 40 years ago, a small group of poor farmers gathered on the prairie not far north of Calgary. What had attracted them there was another small group of workmen clustered around a huge metal tower. Just before the sun went down, a shout went up: "Oil!" Calgary had struck it rich.

The province of Alberta, named for Queen Victoria's daughter, was one of the last parts of North America to be settled by Europeans. It officially became a part of the Canadian Confederation in 1905, with a population that included an unusually high percentage of American immigrants who had been lured there toward the end of the 19th century by an intensive promotion campaign. The early settlers looked for oil, and some of them found a little,

but mainly they made their living as ranchers and farmers in a very rough environment.

The debates over energy and separatism, like the hammering out of the new constitution, may take a long time, and the outcome is anybody's guess. But one thing is absolutely certain about them: the fighting will be done with words, not bullets, and the words will be politely delivered. More than most of the world's peoples, Canadians are very highly civilized.

It may very well be a result of the fact that Canada is more a nation of independent provinces, each with its own character, holding the uniting force of a strong central government at arm's length. It gives the people a strong feeling of individuality, and with it a strong respect for the rights of other individuals. In Canada, local government is stronger than central government with the result that average citizens are closer to their government and therefore, apparently, more respectful of its rules.

Whatever the reason, Canadians are more aware of their collective responsibilities than most other national groups; dramatically more so than Americans.

It's a thing that never fails to impress Americans when they visit cities like Montreal and Toronto, which are squeaky-clean compared to New York or Los Angeles. In Toronto, about the only graffiti in the town is on the campus of the University of Toronto, unless a purist wants to consider the "Post No Bills" signs (scrupulously obeyed!) that appear on construction fences all over the city.

Compared to New York, the largest city in the United States, Canada's largest city, Toronto, spends just about half as much per capita on garbage collection, but the difference in results is nothing short of dramatic. A University of Toronto sociologist claims it's because Canadians have "a greater deference to authority and a feeling that the streets belong to everybody." In other societies, she points out, "...one feels the streets belong to no one. They are no man's land."

The deference to authority goes beyond clean streets. A New Yorker in Toronto once said he was absolutely amazed by the fact that "everybody waits for the light to turn green!" And the crime statistics would make any country proud. Handguns must be registered and it's far from easy to buy one. Assassination is unheard of, and the annual murder rate is actually going down each year. Occasionally a major crime shocks the nation, as happened the time a police officer was shot and killed in the line of duty. It resulted in a major conference of police from all over Canada to discuss ways of preventing such a thing from happening again. During one of the debates over whether bulletproof vests ought to be standard issue for policemen, representatives of the constabulary from Newfoundland caucused to consider the question of whether this might be the time for them to begin carrying guns.

During the years the West was being won, people in Boston and Philadelphia were lionising characters like Jesse James and Billy the Kid, who were cutting a swath through the American West robbing banks, stagecoaches or any citizen who seemed likely to trade a few dollars for the removal of the threat of a six-gun. In Montreal and Quebec the heroes of the day were the men of the Northwest Mounted Police…"The Mounties."

It was inevitable that they would become heroes to Americans, too. Nelson Eddy helped when he wooed Jeanette McDonald in the movie "Indian Love Call," even though to red-blooded American and Canadian boys, his portrayal, with all that singing and love stuff, put the lie to the image they preferred, that of a rugged do-gooder who would brave arctic ice and snow, saloons full of desperate men, dense forests and high mountains to get his man. It was his job, his calling, his sacred duty to "*always* get his man." But if Nelson Eddy seemed more intent on getting his woman, and Sergeant Preston of the Yukon and his faithful sled dog, "King" seemed to go out of his way to court danger, the image of the red-coated Mountie still inspires awe in outsiders and pride in the hearts of Canadians.

The West was truly wild before the first force of 300 Mounties began patrolling the 300,000 square-mile North West Territories in 1873. Trappers representing three different competing companies were ranging through the area and were often at each others' throats. Together they faced often hostile Indians, who were sometimes supplied with firewater and firepower by smugglers from across the United States border.

Officials in Lower Canada secured legislation from London in 1803 that allowed them to appoint peace officers for the Indian Territories. They would be empowered to make arrests and haul the perpetrators back to Montreal for trial. The problem was that the only white men in Indian country were trappers and fur traders who were competing with each other for business. Since the law allowed anyone to make an arrest, it proved to be a handy way for many of them to eliminate the competition.

By 1821, The Hudson's Bay Company had emerged as the only trader in the fur business and became responsible for law and order. Life was quiet for a while, but life in the West was changing. The fur trade was declining, which was bad news for the white man. The buffalo herds were thinning out, which was handwriting on the wall for the Indian. And plans were being made to build a railroad that would bring more settlers from the East. That didn't make anyone already there too happy, and the prospect of coming change made everyone a little edgy and restless. The stage was set for new trouble.

One of the prime movers in the transcontinental railroad idea was Canada's first Prime Minister, Sir John A. Macdonald. In an attempt to give his railroad a secure destination, he ordered the creation of a new and different kind of police force. It began with handbills distributed in the Eastern cities looking for men between the ages of 18 and 40 years, "…of sound constitution, able to ride, active and able-bodied, of good character." There was no mention of high adventure in the offering, but the first recruits undoubtedly had that in mind. They certainly weren't lured by the pay, which was 75 cents a day for recruits and a raise to a dollar a day for men promoted to constable. But there was another inducement. If a man could live through three years out there, he could claim 160 acres of the Territory for his own.

No one really knows why, but there were more than 1,500 applicants for those first 300 jobs. It was a lucky break for George A. French, a former British lieutenant colonel, who had been handed the job of selecting the men and then training them for their new jobs.

It was a police force run along military lines, and a lot of attention was given to appearance. Their horses, all very handsome, were especially selected for them; each man carried a well-cared-for carbine and at his side, in a highly-polished holster, a long-barrelled revolver. From his white helmet with its shiny brass fittings to his gleaming black boots, every man was smartly turned out in the spit and polish tradition of the British Army. Even their scarlet jackets conspired to make them look for all the world like a military unit from England out to impress "the locals" in some corner of the Empire. The difference in this case was that these *were* the locals, but as well-trained as any unit ever sent out from the Mother Country.

But what about those scarlet jackets? When Britain sent soldiers to put down a rebellion in its North American colonies, she discovered that war was a bit different on this side of the Atlantic, and red coats made soldiers good targets for an enemy concealed in the forest. Now, just short of 100 years later, they seemed determined to make the same mistake again. But this time it was no mistake.

This was no army marching off to war, this was a peace-keeping force and they were determined to use peaceful means to do the job. The red coats were part of it. They wanted the Indians to find them and they wanted to make it absolutely clear that they were not the same kind of people as the American troops who had been making life miserable for Indians on the Great Plains. The American soldiers wore *blue* jackets.

Just before winter arrived in 1873, three troops of 50 men each arrived at Lower Fort Garry, not far north of Winnipeg. They were under orders to continue their training through the winter and be ready to begin showing the flag on the prairies when spring came. The following June a second force of about 200 men was sent out by train via Chicago to Fargo, North Dakota, where they would assemble and march north to rendezvous with the others, then move on out to bring peace to Western Canada.

When the trains arrived in Fargo, the locals turned out to meet them and to have a joke or two at their expense. The Canadians gave them more to laugh about than they had expected. The equipment to supply this little army had been loaded into freight cars in Toronto as it had been received. No one had thought to sort it first. The scene in Fargo turned to chaos as the men unloaded the cars, and even the most sympathetic American could see that it would take them more than a week to get all that gear in order.

It may have taken longer than that, in fact, but these men were under the command of a former British Army officer. Lieutenant-Colonel French got his men organized and by the morning of the second day they were at work getting the equipment organized. By mid-afternoon that same day, the first division marched proudly out of town. The second left early that evening and the third was on its way the following day.

No one in Fargo believed what they saw. They had no way of knowing that what they were seeing was only the beginning of a tradition that would grow to one of the great legends of the West.

That summer, the Mounties marched across the prairie in full uniform, each division mounted on different color horses. They were riding out to establish forts, and did, in fact, set up four of them that formed a square across the plains. But they were also on a mission to impress the Indians that law and order was coming to the Wild West.

The strategy was to go into territory claimed by the proudest and most warlike of the tribes and win their

confidence by talking with them. Their early attempts were mildly successful, but the most powerful tribe, the Blackfeet, seemed to prefer to watch and wait. The Mounties knew they were being watched and quietly went about their business. They could wait, too.

Meanwhile, the whiskey smugglers, many of whom had been tracked down by the new police, began whispering to the Blackfeet that the redcoats were more of a threat to the Indian than the American Cavalry ever had been. But Crowfoot, the most powerful of the chiefs, had some experience with whiskey smugglers in the past and believed that anything they said was most likely a lie. That convinced him he ought to go have a talk with the newcomers.

During the formal pow-wow, Crowfoot was impressed by the honesty and dignity of these white men. He had seen them at work, too, and was already impressed by that. Within days he spread the word to the other chiefs that the man he had spoken with, Assistant Commissioner J.M. Macleod, was a white man who "...knows no fear, whose favor no money can buy, yet who is indeed the Indians' friend."

Much later, Crowfoot was pleased to say that his original impression of the Mounties had been accurate. "If the police had not come to this country," he said, "where would we all be now? Bad men and whiskey were killing us so fast that few of us would have been left today. The police have protected us as the feathers of a bird protect it from the frosts of winter."

Down in the United States, the Army wasn't quite as interested in protecting the Indian. It was in their best interests, they felt, to kill them off. The war went on for more than a dozen years with huge losses on both sides, finally reaching a climax when the great Sioux chief, Sitting Bull, gathered the biggest Indian force in history at the Little Big Horn River, not far south of the Canadian border. They were met there, on the hundredth anniversary of American Independence, by the United States Seventh Cavalry, commanded by George A. Custer. The American force was slaughtered to the last man, and a few months later Sitting Bull retreated with his army to the safety of Canada.

Though the Sioux were weary of war by that point, it was clear to the Force that it was only a matter of time before they would be ready to make trouble again. The Mounties, all 214 of them who had been assigned to patrol the 700-mile border, sent word back East that they had "massed" themselves against the Sioux and there wasn't a thing to worry about. Counting women and children, there were more than 5,000 new Indians to deal with and no one was sure if the Blackfoot chiefs would join with them.

The answer was to impress the Sioux with the idea that a lone rider in a scarlet tunic was a man to be respected and obeyed. The first step in that direction was taken by Inspector J.M. Walsh, who took four men and two scouts into the heart of Sitting Bull's camp and calmly asked for a council to explain to the newcomers that this country was the realm of the Queen and that he, as the Queen's representative, expected her laws to be obeyed.

No white man had ever done anything like that before. No white man had ever earned the respect of Sitting Bull before, either. Later, when the Americans tried to negotiate with him for peace, Sitting Bull agreed to talk with them, but only after he was assured that the only soldiers present would be the police in scarlet jackets.

Crowfoot, the Blackfoot Chief, had long since added to the Mounties' image in the eyes of the Sioux. When they asked him to join in their fight against the white man, he quickly refused. When they threatened him with war if he didn't join them, he told them he wasn't worried because he knew the Redcoats would protect his people just as they had always done.

But Indians weren't the only people the Mounties had to think about. White settlers were arriving in increasing numbers, and it was up to the constables to take care of them, even including delivering their mail. They were forced to settle land disputes as peacefully as possible, to help the sick, rescue the stranded and to keep the railroad moving west on schedule in spite of strikes and Indian opposition. And they did it all with almost no bloodshed.

The gold rush in the Yukon in 1896, one of the wildest ever, drew a contingent of Mounties to keep the peace. Superintendent S.B. Steele, who commanded the fewer-than-300 officers and men from Dawson City, described it as "about the roughest place on earth." Not only were the settlements in the grip of thieves and murderers, but the weather during the winter and spring of 1898 was rough even by Yukon standards. From March 3 until May 1, the Territory was hit by a blizzard that stopped only once or twice during the whole period. By the time the sun came out again, the snow was more than 60 feet deep. But through it all, gold-hungry prospectors kept coming up through Skagway and over the mountain passes into Canada. And through it all, bands of men Steele called "ruffians," roamed the mountain looking for trouble. It was up to the Mounties to see that they didn't find it.

Just before the storm ended, a landslide on the American side killed 72 people, and the job of carrying out the dead fell to the Mounties. Being a Mountie is that kind of job.

By the turn of the century, the Force was well-established in the Yukon and had moved north into the Northwest Territory where they established "the most northerly police post in the world" at Herschel Island in the Beaufort Sea. Their Commissioner was proud to report in 1904 that his men were "...today dealing with all classes of men – the lawless element on the border, the cowboys and Indians on the plains, the coal miners in the mountains, the gold miners in the Yukon, and the American whalers and the Esquimaux in Hudson Bay and the far distant Arctic Sea."

The world was impressed. So was the new King of England, Edward VII who, on June 24, 1904, "knighted" the Force and changed its name to The Royal North-West Mounted Police. Less than 20 years later, they joined with the Dominion Police to become what they are today, The Royal Canadian Mounted Police.

Today's Mountie is more likely to have a snowmobile than a dog sled and a car or a helicopter gets him around a lot more easily than a horse ever did. The Force has grown from the original 300 men to more than 18,000, and the pay is a bit higher than the original 75 cents a day, but the tradition is as strong as it ever has been.

In the Yukon Territory, where the tradition proved to be so valuable less than a century ago, 90 Mounties patrol an area well over twice as big as the entire United Kingdom. Like their partners in the Canadian Provinces, they do the work of a highway patrol, local police, F.B.I., Scotland Yard, secret service, park ranger, delivery man or midwife.

As their chief superintendent likes to point out, there are fewer people in the Yukon than some other parts of Canada, so there is naturally less crime. Distance is still a problem, of course, but he's proud to report that the RCMP has access to computers and satellite communication that makes getting their man a whole lot easier than it once was.

There were three murders committed in the Yukon in all of 1978. One of the suspected killers was apprehended in Florida when he was stopped for speeding by a highway patrol unit that had picked up a message from the RCMP. Years ago, by the time a Mountie heard about a crime, got to the scene, made his investigation, effected his arrest and found a judge to try the case, it could take as long as two years for justice to be done.

Modern technology makes other parts of the job more

effective, too. Radio repeaters scattered through the Territory make it possible for the Mounties to keep in radio contact with their headquarters. They also make it possible for them to keep in contact with their families when they're out in the wilderness, which is often.

"The only thing I never do out here," reports one of them, "is write parking tickets." A typical day can begin with an appearance in court on a traffic case and end with an evening's conversation in a trappers' chilly cabin high in the mountains. A big part of the job is still "showing the flag," and the routine patrols through thousands of miles of wilderness can become a dangerous job. It's a country that doesn't forgive mistakes and any Mountie who wants to collect his retirement pay knows he'd better not make any. Before leaving on a patrol, he files an itinerary, which he's careful not to change any more than necessary, and packs extra supplies just in case the plan does get changed. As he makes his rounds, he makes it a point to stop at every house and cabin he passes. "In the cities," one of them explained, "no one ever wants to see a policeman, but out here, they're insulted if you don't stop." The visits are valuable on both sides. The Mountie brings news and the latest jokes, sometimes he brings the mail, always he brings companionship; a thing often in short supply out in the wilderness. In return, he gets a feel for anything unusual that may be happening out there. And the more often he makes his rounds, the less often anything unusual does happen.

From the very first, the major source of interest in Canada by European adventurers and businessmen was the possibility that there was a water route through it to the fabulous East. A lot of men died trying to find it, a lot of others died convinced there was no such thing. By the beginning of the 20th century, nobody cared much whether a North West Passage existed, and explorers turned their attention to a new challenge: being first to reach the North Pole. Several attempts were made, and each contributed to knowledge of Canada's vast northland. Finally, after three tries, Robert E. Peary made the Pole on April 6, 1909.

Once that had been accomplished, other Arctic explorers turned their energies to exploring and mapping the Arctic Islands. The Norwegian Roald Amundsen had made an interesting discovery in 1903 when he made his way in a herring boat from Norway to the Pacific Ocean across the top of Canada. There was a North West Passage after all. But the world was so excited about reaching the Pole, nobody bothered to duplicate his trip until 1940, when a small ship belonging to the Royal Canadian Mounted Police sailed through the Passage from Vancouver to Halifax. Four years later, she made the return trip, becoming the first vessel to make the Passage in both directions.

But even now, not many ships ever pass in the Arctic night. There are easier ways to get to the exotic East these days, and the only incentive to steam through the ice floes has been to see if it might be a practical way to get oil from Alaska to the East Coast of the United States. It isn't.

In 1670, finding a North West Passage would have been a feat closely comparable, even preferable to some, to finding the Holy Grail. In the spring of that year, England's King Charles II granted a charter creating a company grandly called the "Governor and Company of Adventurers trading into Hudson's Bay." It didn't take long to shorten that down to the "Hudson's Bay Company," and modern Canadians have shortened it further still to "The Bay."

The charter gave a trade monopoly to a group of 18 merchants and noblemen headed by the King's cousin, Prince Rupert, and made them "true and absolute Lordes and Proprietors" of all the territory draining into Hudson Bay. The Bay itself is bigger than France and England combined, the land involved is bigger than the area covered by the Mediterranean Sea.

The King had no idea what he was giving away. But he did know he had to establish a presence in Northern Canada. Henry Hudson and others had explored the territory and claimed it for England. Samuel de Champlain and others had done some exploring, too, and they claimed what they saw for France. By forming the Hudson's Bay Company, Charles thought he could take away some of the fur trade for his own people and keep the French at bay. Most important, though, he wanted England to be the power to find the North West Passage.

But just being there wasn't enough. Prince Rupert's Company lost no time building trading posts along the rivers where it would be easy for the Indians to reach them. So there was no mistaking who they were, they raised their personal flag over the posts. Actually, it was a British Union Jack. What made it their personal flag was the monogram "H.B.C." added to the lower right-hand corner. No private company, before or since, has ever used the British flag as its own trademark. It's one of the perks you get if you're the king's favorite cousin.

It was just another red flag to the French, though, and an unofficial war quickly broke out between the trappers from the south and the newcomers from London. It became an official war seven years later, and for more than a dozen years the Hudson's Bay trading posts alternately fell and were recaptured. Mostly they were in French hands.

It went on like that for years, but the British aren't characterized as bulldogs for nothing. Even when all their posts but one were occupied by the French and the Company had stopped paying dividends to its shareholders, a drought that lasted more than 20 years, it went right on exploring its private country and searching for that North West Passage.

In 1689, a 19-year-old lad named Henry Kelsey slipped past the hostile French and marched 200 miles north from the Churchill River to see if he could find some friendly Indians. He didn't find any, so the following year he went west along the Hayes and Saskatchewan rivers. He didn't come back for two more years, but his trip took him more than 600 miles into the prairies and he became the first white man to see buffalo herds in Manitoba.

The French, meanwhile, weren't exactly sitting on their haunches. By 1730, the Hudson's Bay Company had entrenched itself in the North and the French businessmen in Montreal decided to entrench themselves in the West. They dispatched Sieur La Verendrye to take charge of their western outposts and to do a little exploring on the side. In the process, he discovered the mouth of the Saskatchewan River and probably pushed west far enough to have his breath taken away by the sight of the Rocky Mountains.

The prospect of French competition goaded the Hudson's Bay Company into moving west, too, and two years later they dispatched Anthony Henday to take their flag inland. The trip made him the official discoverer of the Canadian Rockies and made the Company richer still as they used information he brought back to establish posts in present-day Saskatchewan and Alberta. Parliament went right along with them, giving them grants to lands in the West and the North, making all of Canada, except the colonies along the St. Lawrence and the Great Lakes, the exclusive property of The Bay.

When the British defeated the French at Quebec and New France ceased to exist, it seemed as though the world had finally been made safe for the Hudson's Bay Company. They had long since gained the confidence of the Indians by offering them better-quality goods for their furs. It was a shrewd business move made even better by the fact that the goods they traded were things like steel knives and iron kettles, things the Indians came to think of as the bare necessities of life. The Bay also got a lot of mileage out of heavy wool blankets bordered with red, green and yellow stripes. In the cold north, nothing could have been more perfect. They were such a popular item, in fact, the Company still makes and sells them. They've become almost as much a symbol of Canada as hockey players and maple leaves.

Once the French threat was eliminated, Scotsmen who had been lurking in the eastern maritime areas decided to go into the fur business themselves. The Bay officially looked down its collective nose at these adventurers they scornfully called "pedlars," and generally regarded them as small-timers. Most of the "Adventurers of England" who ran the Company never left England and the men they put in charge of their trading posts generally never left their fortified places of business. They were big enough to hire other men to do the exploring and dealing on the frontier. But their new competition wasn't and, in spite of what The Bay may have thought, that was an advantage.

As small businessmen, the Scots were in the thick of the trade in person. They took over the routes abandoned by the French voyageurs with a spirit of fierce competition the French had never dreamed of. They even competed with each other and that helped keep The Bay complacent.

Finally they banded together in a confederation they called the North West Company and at last the Adventurers of England sat up and took notice. The Bay sent Samuel Hearne up to explore its northern territory. The trip took him all the way to the Arctic Ocean and took everyone's imagination to new heights over the prospect of the biggest cache of furs ever found on the North American continent. The king had already given the Arctic lands to his cousin and his adventuresome friends, but the riches there would actually belong to anyone who got there first.

The Nor'Westers caught The Bay flatfooted when they sent an American named Peter Pond to set up a trading post near Lake Athabasca at the top of present-day Alberta and Saskatchewan. It was virgin territory in 1778 and the furs Pond brought out over the next few years made a lot of men like the Frobisher brothers and John and James McGill very rich. Pond finally went back to the United States almost penniless after having tried to become more than just a hired hand for the North West Company, and he learned a thing or two about making business deals with Scotsmen.

The North West Company grew and prospered for the rest of the 18th century and through a dozen years into the 19th. Their downfall seems to have come as a result of forgetting the most common Scottish stereotype: thrift.

The Hudson's Bay Company had been growing during those years, too, but its directors even after years of taking no dividends, were content with a small return on their "investment." Their competitors took their profits and left very little in the till to keep the company going. In their defense, the Scots traders had seen this vast country and felt there was no end to the riches out there. But with lawsuits to settle, brushfire wars to fight between themselves, and a growing number of employees necessary to match the competition, running a Canadian fur business had become a very expensive proposition. Without competition, of course, costs could be much more easily controlled, and so, in 1821, the two companies agreed to join together and the Hudson's Bay Company swallowed up its competitor.

With its monopoly secure, there was nowhere for The Bay to go but up. They eliminated trading posts that were too close together and established new ones where there seemed to be opportunities for higher profits. In the process, they become operators of trading posts in the St. Lawrence area, in Labrador, along the Great Lakes, in the Oregon territory, in Alaska and just about everywhere in between. And in return for the furs they took out of Alaska, they agreed to export grain to Russia, satisfying a need the Russians are still feeling a century and a half later.

Naturally, the fur traders didn't foresee that any more than they foresaw that some day men of fashion in Europe would consider their Paris Beaus, their Wellingtons or Regents made from beaver skins old hat. The new hat in the 1840s was made of silk and there simply was no way to raise silkworms in the Northwest. The market for beaver had held up well for almost 200 years, not a bad record for fashion, and the trappers had found a good life, for them, in the process.

But in all that time they had hardly changed the landscape at all, and the land in Western Canada was as hostile as it ever had been.

Some people had tried to establish farms on the prairies, but generally gave it up as a bad job in the face of droughts, windstorms, unbelievably cold winters, locusts and even gophers. The result was that by the time of Canadian Confederation in 1867, there were only about 25,000 white men in all of Canada west of Toronto. Most of them were trappers working for the Hudson's Bay Company who had fallen on relatively hard times.

South of the border, Americans were streaming into the West answering a call they referred to as "Manifest Destiny," a call from God Himself to tame the wilderness and settle the continent. Officials in Ottawa knew it was only a matter of time before the call lured them into the Canadian wilderness, too, and the only way to head the Americans off was to give Canadians their own destiny and make it easy for them to settle the West.

The first step was to send Government agents west to survey the land and establish towns that would become new homes for farmers from Ontario. The Hudson's Bay Company had already traded off most of its land rights to the new Government, work had begun on the coast-to-coast railroad, and the Mounties were in place to protect everyone's basic rights. But there was a problem no one had considered: the rights of the people already there.

The Indian "problem" had been defused, they thought, by a series of treaties that quietly herded them off to reservations in the North. The real problem, as it turned out, was another race of men in the Canadian West, neither Indian nor white. They called themselves Métis. There were some 6000 of them, about ten times the number of white men on the prairie, and they had been there since their French ancestors had followed Champlain into North America and decided to stay. They intermarried with the Indians to create a new stock out of the best traits of both. The Métis had existed for more than 100 years as nomadic buffalo hunters and considered the establishment of Manitoba a threat to their future. Another threat came in the form of settlers and buffalo hunters on the American plains. By 1876, the southern herd had been wiped out and the northern herd didn't come back from its winter migration. The handwriting had been on the wall for a long time and bad blood had built up between the British settlers from Ontario, who were mostly Protestant, and the Métis, most of whom were fiercely Catholic.

The Métis were an easy-going race, but not so docile that they weren't capable of fighting back. There had been several incidents between them and the new settlers, but the situation came to a head in 1869, when the Métis found a leader in the person of Louis Riel, who turned away a government surveying party near the Red River and ordered them never to return. To make sure they wouldn't, he barricaded the only road and then took over the main Hudson's Bay Company fort in the area in a move that so amazed the Bay's governor that the takeover was accomplished without a single shot being fired.

Then he established *La Nation Métisse* and began petitioning the Ottawa Government for guarantees of their rights. His pleas were largely ignored. The Prime Minister was sure that the tide of immigration of "real Canadians" would before long leave the half-breeds far outnumbered and more docile. But he didn't know much about half-breeds or about Riel, who was building a huge following among his people and finally declared war on Canada in 1885.

He won the first few battles, but it was inevitable that he would lose the war. Within two months Riel surrendered in the face of an overwhelming army sent out from Ottawa, but many of his followers kept on fighting anyway. Hope ran out on them in just a few weeks and Riel was taken to Regina and hanged for his trouble.

The soldiers who defeated him had made the trip from the East in just 11 days, a feat that convinced the Government once and for all that it should finance the last links in the transcontinental railroad. They moved as quickly as their army, and the last spike was driven on November 7, 1885, less than 10 days before Reil was hanged. He probably neither knew that his rebellion made the finished railroad possible nor how that would transform Manitoba from a stepchild of the Confederation into a desirable destination for settlers from the East.

The railroad was good for the Hudson's Bay Company, too. The general right-of-way took the line from one trading post to another, conveniently connecting them for the first time. Towns grew around them, of course, and little by little The Bay downgraded its fur-trading operations and converted many of the old trading posts into department stores. They referred to themselves as "Harrod's on the Prairie," and carefully copied the famous London store in design as well as in merchandise. It was a great idea, but their pioneer customers passed over the fine china and other touches of elegance the proprietors in England really believed would be in demand anywhere at all.

But if their merchandising skills weren't finely-honed, they were willing to learn, and they put the best minds they could find to work to turn The Bay into a major force in retailing. The reorganization, a tribute to British conservatism in business, went on for 50 years before any major changes were made. The stores went right on selling British elegance in dark, but very dignified showrooms. They continued to stock merchandise that was all but useless in the rough-and-tumble West. But they survived, God bless 'em, and brought a little style to the place in the process.

Finally, as recently as 1970, when the Company was 300 years old, they decided it was time to wheel out their new look and catch up with the 20th century. One of the first steps was to move the Company's headquarters from London to Winnipeg, another was to call themselves in advertising what their customers had been calling them for generations. It was acceptable for the first time for the Company to call *itself* "The Bay."

The changes are obvious to anyone who shops The Bay today. Its stores are as modern as any in the world, and you can as easily buy a polyester blouse as a fur-lined parka in the smallest of them. But some of the stores are still trading posts, especially in the far North where they accept furs in trade for merchandise on occasion and where the inventory gets replaced once a year when the ice melts just the same as in the original posts three centuries ago.

It takes about five days to travel by train from Halifax on the East Coast to Vancouver on the West, not much longer than it took the first transcontinental Pacific Express to make the trip from Toronto to Port Moody, British Columbia, in the spring of 1886. Most travellers these days make the trip from Montreal to Vancouver just for the fun of it. And the journey has become one of the most famous rides in the world.

VIA Rail Canada, as the combined Canadian Pacific and Canadian National Railways is now called, offers all kinds of special tours ranging from combination train and boat trips to car rental service along the way to treats for backpackers. But the demand for roomettes or bedrooms on the regular transcontinental runs is tremendous and people who don't book them months in advance usually don't get the accommodation. And there's a very good reason for it: there are few better ways to get an idea of the beauty of Canada and few better railroads anywhere in the world.

The first train to make the trip left Toronto at 5:00 in the afternoon on June 28, 1886 and reached British Columbia at noon on July 4th. If the trip is unforgettable today, it was a genuine adventure back then. The average speed of the train worked out to be just under 21 miles an hour. It would have been faster except for a trestle that nearly collapsed under the train's weight at one point and what railroad officials described as "a slight landslide" at another.

It didn't take them long to get all the kinks ironed out of the system, and by Queen Victoria's birthday, in the spring of 1887, the western destination had been moved to a brand-new city called Vancouver, where the railroad had built a fine new hotel to make it a more attractive destination.

The railroad had built some other hotels along the right-of-way, too. The idea was not so much to provide destinations as rest stops along the way. In a bid for business, they had built unusually elaborate and comfortable passenger cars.

The berths were longer and wider than the ones George Pullman was building for the American railroads and the woodwork and brass fittings inside and out conspired to make the passenger cars quite a bit heavier. A good part of the transcontinental run was uphill, which put a strain on the locomotives and the addition of dining cars to the Canadian Pacific trains was just too much of an added strain. Rest stops were the answer, but these were no ordinary establishments. The original line had three, each carefully chosen for its spectacular location. When passengers stretched their legs at a Canadian Pacific rest stop they were usually reluctant to get back on the train. It wasn't long before the three railside restaurants, Mount Stephen House, Glacier House and Fraser Canyon House became full-fledged hotels and they were followed quickly by hotels at Banff and Lake Louise. The railroaders had discovered a very interesting sideline.

Once they had spread their rails across North America, they set their sights on spanning the world, and by the time the first train arrived in Vancouver, they had already built a pier there that would serve steamers bound for Hong Kong and Japan across the Pacific, forming a link in what they dreamed would be an around-the-world British rail system. They hadn't considered the relatively slow service from Britain to Canada's East Coast, nor the competition already established in the Pacific. But their Pacific fleet became one of the fastest and best in the business. It was possible to mail a letter in Quebec and be assured it would arrive in Hong Kong less than 30 days later. And if the letter was an order for a few tons of tea, Canadians on the East Coast would probably be drinking it less than 3 months later.

Flushed with success like that, the Canadian Pacific went to the public with a proposition that they could sail on the maiden voyage of new, British-built ships they had ordered and in the process take an around-the-world cruise. It was an unheard-of scheme back in 1891 and a first of its kind. Even more unheard-of was the price: "Around the World in 80 Days for $600!"

In their advertising for the first transcontinental train ride, the CP's promoters said it was "A Red Letter Day For Canada." Looking back on it, no one can deny it.

The railroad was not only good for business, it was indispensable to western expansion. By the time it was finished, it seemed well-worth the effort and expense. But what an effort it was! Crossing the prairies from Winnipeg to the mountains was one of the great construction feats of the century. They laid steel rails imported from England and Germany across a 962-mile stretch in about 18 months

with almost no delays. The tracklayers were a little unnerved by the lines of Indians who sat cross-legged in the grass scrutinizing their every move, but their hostility didn't extend much beyond pulling up surveyors' pegs or setting up tepees on the completed track sections. The Mounties managed to keep that threat in check, but nobody could do anything about the obstacle Mother Nature had put in their path: the Rocky Mountains.

The line climbed the Rockies along the same route as the Bow River, which took it to the top of the Great Divide at an altitude of 5,337 feet. What goes up must come down, of course, and the trip down the western slope was longer and a good bit steeper. At one point, the drop was over a thousand feet in less than seven miles. Taking a train up the hill was a problem solved by adding a few more locomotives and a lot more patience. But westbound trains had to go downhill, which is a horse of quite another color. The builders installed special spurs along the way so a runaway train could be diverted into an uphill direction, which would presumably spend its energy. Trains were required to come to a full stop at each of them for a brake inspection and the brakes were checked again at the bottom; a process that generally took time because of the heat the brake shoes built up on the way down.

The trip wasn't over at that point, of course. There were deep canyons to span, avalanche areas to skirt, glaciers to avoid. It all added up to a nightmare for the railroad's builders, but for travelers who use the line, it created one of the most spectacularly beautiful trips in the world.

When the railroad was finished, Canada was in the midst of a depression, but the Canadian Pacific kept growing anyway under the leadership of William C. Van Horn, an American who had crossed the border in 1881 and never went back. During his 25 years as head of the railroad he added new lines and replaced old ones with more modern embankments and bridges. He made the railroad a symbol of a united Canada.

Turning the depression to his advantage, he encouraged unemployed people to look for a new life in the West, where they could grow wheat to serve a world market which could be reached, incidentally, by his railroad. He turned out-of-work buffalo hunters into friends by paying them to collect buffalo skeletons which he shipped, by rail of course, back east to be made into fertilizer to be shipped west again to make the wheat farms more productive.

Not many details escaped his eye. He once noted that a wooden freight car weighed some 900 pounds more when it was new than it did a year or so later when the green wood had dried out. He encouraged his people to get the tare weight marked as quickly as possible when a car was new and then take as long as possible to correct it. "...It will result in our carrying a very considerable amount of freight for nothing," he wrote. Occasionally mistakes were made in planning in spite of Van Horne's eagle eye. When the Banff Springs Hotel was built, for instance, it somehow got turned in the wrong direction and the most beautiful view from the ground floor was from the back of the building where the kitchens were. Even a master railroad builder couldn't turn the building around, but Van Horne solved the problem by adding a pavilion to the back of the building so his guests wouldn't be disappointed.

Guests at the hotels he built were rarely disappointed, nor are they today, and their architectural style set the pace for nearly all major construction in Canada for generations. The railroad got into the hotel business with its mountain rest stops, but it didn't become big business until the railroad acquired building lots in the little town of Vancouver which it sold and used the profits to build the elegant hotel there. The profits were big enough to build the original Hotel Vancouver as well as an equally elegant railroad station and the finest opera house on the West Coast of North America – and there was still money left over.

Not being one to let money lie idle, Van Horne turned his sights back inland. Railroad surveyors had discovered wonderful, hot springs in the heart of the Rockies in a spot that is beautiful even by Canadian standards. One of them named it Banff after a county in Scotland. Van Horne put architect Bruce Price to work designing a five-story hotel there. Price turned to Scotland for his inspiration and built a structure reminiscent of a Scottish highland castle. Even if it faced the wrong way it was a big hit, and later additions have corrected any defects the original may have had. Today it's in the center of a national park, which assures that the views of snow-capped mountains and crystal-clear lakes won't change any time soon. And fantastic skiing possibilities have turned it from a summer resort into a year-round enterprise.

Not long after that he added the Chateau Lake Louise to the chain and instituted a custom still followed there: to wake guests who request it in time to catch the sunrise over the lake. Many people say it's unquestionably the most beautiful sight in the world, even if does often occur at four in the morning.

When ferry service was established between the City of Vancouver and Vancouver Island, the railroad decided to make Victoria the "end of the line" for the Canadian Pacific

and built the great Gothic Empress Hotel in a park they had created on the waterfront. It was clearly intended to be an outpost of the British Empire, and High Tea is still served there every afternoon at four. That's not to say it's an old-fashioned place, though. At four in the morning there's plenty of activity at the hotel's discotheque.

But the Canadian Pacific's hotel ventures weren't all confined to the West, nor to following British tradition. In 1893 they built the most talked-about hotel in all of North America, overlooking the St. Lawrence River in Quebec. The impression, fittingly, is French Renaissance, and there are few chateaux in France that are as impressive as the Chateau Frontenac.

It was designed by the same Bruce Price who had done the railroad's other hotels and a great many of its terminal buildings, and this building is far and away his best work. To make sure it would be, Van Horne was looking over the architect's shoulder almost every step of the way, even to the point of rowing him out into the river to see for himself if the site was majestic enough for what he had in mind. It surely was. It was the site selected by the original governors of New France as their place of residence. Their Chateau St. Louis had been magnificent, built to impress the New World with their power and affluence, but it was puny by comparision with the structure that replaced it.

From its turrets to its copper roof to its imposing brick walls, it would be magnificent anywhere. But everything it gives to Quebec City, the city gives back in the form of the setting on a bluff high over the river. It's still the center of the city's life, and it's still one of North America's best examples of Old World charm, fortunately with New World comforts unobtrusively blended in.

Though it branched out into the hotel business, the mineral business, the real estate business and almost any other business that could turn a profit, the Canadian Pacific was a railroad first and foremost and it had a strong competitor in that business: the Canadian National Railway, one of the original railroads of the world. The first line ran from St. John about 15 miles across the countryside to connect with the nearest point on the St. Lawrence River at a small town called Laprairie. In 1836, one of the first locomotives built by the Robert Stephenson Company in England arrived in Montreal ready to go to work. It came complete with what may have been the last of the indentured servants sent to the New World. The Company had thoughtfully provided an engineer who, realizing that English rules didn't apply in this particular colony, headed west before the locomotive was unloaded from the ship.

But the Canadians in charge didn't let that get them down. If they could build a railroad, they could drive a train, and the little engine was hooked up to a string of coaches and some flat cars and outfitted with benches for its maiden run. Some 300 of Canada's most influential people, including John Molson, heir to a brewery that had been thriving for more than 40 years by then, and his partners in the railroad, got on board and sat back waiting for the train to take them from Laprairie down to St. John. The locomotive huffed and puffed and huffed some more, but the train didn't budge. Finally, one of the dignitaries stepped down from the coach and announced that the train didn't move because it was too heavy for the engine to pull. But it was not for nothing that he was known as a dignitary. No one would have to be bumped from the train's maiden trip, he told them. It would simply be divided into sections, with the Stephenson locomotive pulling two coaches and the rest being hauled over the line by teams of horses.

The trip took two hours and the idea took Montreal by storm. The railroad had been built to make hauling freight faster and more efficient than the traditional water routes, but shipping by rail wasn't cheaper and the river was as busy as ever. But the promise of high adventure rolling over the rails at unheard-of speeds as much as 20 miles an hour turned everybody on, and if its freight business was disappointing, the Champlain and St. Lawrence Railroad had more passenger business than it cared to handle. The railroad offered a package deal that carried passengers one way by rail and got them home by steamboat on the river. Not only did passengers get to experience the thrill of speed, but had a chance to regain their composure with a relaxing boat ride and between the two could enjoy a picnic lunch along the railroad's right-of-way.

The public developed a passion for railroads and for the rest of the century dozens of short lines were built, some with nothing more in mind than providing passenger service. Some went out of business, some were consolidated with other lines to form bigger enterprises. But everywhere railroads went they brought prosperity, and their general direction was westward.

It wasn't long before Montreal and Toronto were connected by rail and lines ran south into New England to give Canada access to ice-free ports in winter. Rail routes from Canada went into Detroit and Chicago. But for a variety of reasons, not the least of which was that most railroads ran alongside cheaper canals and rivers, business, though good, was not fantastic.

The answer was to open the Golden West, and the federal government backed the formation of the Canadian Pacific to do the job. The C.P. route ran along the United States border because it was considered too cold further north either for growing wheat or for attracting settlers. And, besides, it seemed like a good idea to set up a barrier that the American railroads wouldn't be able to cross if they decided to expand their influence northward.

But not long after the turn of the century new strains of wheat were developed that could be grown hundreds of miles further north than before and a whole new opportunity opened up. The railroaders who had acquired land in the North decided it was time to lay some tracks of their own across the continent. Some had bought townsites and dreamed of connecting them. The phantom towns averaged about ten miles apart, and fulfilled a need the Canadian Pacific's builders hadn't thought of: they would provide communities with shops and stables, neatly-arranged streets and, of course, a railroad station. But without a railroad they didn't exist as much more than maps to dream over.

For several years the entrepreneurs built feeder lines connecting their little prairie towns with the main line of the railroad further south. Then, in 1908 they began building a main line of their own, a construction feat that would make the Canadian Pacific effort seem easy by comparison.

It took more than a year to move less than 100 miles eastward, and two more years to cut a 2,200-foot tunnel to connect with the new roadbed beyond. It was the end of 1912 before the construction workers reached the Rocky Mountains, 416 miles east of where their line began. Going over the mountains wasn't any easier for these men than it had been for the crews who built the Canadian Pacific, but finally, nine years after work began, Canada had two railroads connecting the Atlantic and Pacific, and a lot of little towns that offered new reasons for more people to move west. It also went a long way toward taming the North.

A lot of people who have never seen Canada visualize it as a wasteland of snow and ice where nobody lives and where temperatures in the summer never get much higher than the low 50s and in winter – which seems to be all the time – the thermometer often goes down past 50-below zero, and stays there.

It's a natural reaction. It's a fair description of the Northwest Territories for an outsider, and the Northwest Territories, after all, cover more than 1.3 million square miles. It's an area about the size of India, which is home to about 547 *million* people. The Northwest Territories has a population of less than 50 *thousand*!

There is a lot of ice in the far-northern part of Canada, but surprisingly little snow. Officially, New York City, which is well-known as a year-round seaport, gets more than 40 inches of snow in an average winter. In Yellowknife, the capital of the Northwest Territories, annual snowfall is just about 10 inches. The difference, of course, is that snow eventually melts in New York, but in Yellowknife it just blows around.

"Your first winter up here, that's the tricky one," said one housewife. It takes some adjustments to get used to the weather, where the wind can blow for days at 100 miles an hours and more, drifting the snow and burying buildings. It takes even more to get attuned to the long nights that can last more than 20 hours some of the time. And possibly worst of all is the need for companionship, and "visiting" is rated number one among all the activities people turn to for making life easier.

If Canada's cities are the cleanest in the world, the towns and cities of the Northwest Territories have a harder time clinging to the image than some others. Huge ravens, smarter than the average bird, apparently, have learned over the years that they can get food from garbage cans and that if enough of them attack one at the same time, they can tip it over and knock the lid off. Then they take off with the bags that fall out and drop them to the ground to break them open. It makes a mess.

The ravens are also a hazard on the golf course at Yellowknife. Yes, they have a golf course at Yellowknife. There's no grass, but partially frozen sand makes quite acceptable turf and, if you can get your ball to the "green" without having it snatched away by a raven, they've added oil to the sand to make it perfect for putting.

The big event of the year on that golf course is the Midnight Golf Tourney. As if the club itself isn't unusual, golfers enter for the novelty of playing under the midnight sun. It's all part of an annual frolic called the Raven Mad Days. If anyone has a right to celebrate the rites of spring, certainly the residents of Yellowknife are among the world's most deserving.

Further north, up near the Arctic Circle, spring isn't quite as noticeable, but for some people it's a time to start thinking about stocking up the larder. Every year in April, housewives on Baffin Island get a catalogue in the mail from their local supermarket, located more than 1,500 miles away in Montreal. They have three or four weeks to shop its pages, but it's important that they have their minds made up before the end of May so their order and their check can be in Montreal in time to get the groceries

together and loaded aboard the only ship that will go up to Baffin Island all year. The shipment may weigh as much as a ton-and-a-half, but it has to last until the boat comes back again a year later, which is how long they'll have to wait for another chance if something was left out of their order.

If there's any frozen food in the consignment, it can be stored on the back porch along with seal and caribou carcasses that provide the mainstay of the local diet. To thaw it slowly, housewives move it indoors to the refrigerator.

It's not as though the little settlements up north only see outsiders once a year. Far from it. There's an airline that runs a regularly-scheduled service across Baffin Island from Frobisher Bay to Pangnirtung three times a week. At least that's what the schedule says. It's a 200-mile flight that can take anywhere from several hours to several days, depending on the weather. Sometimes it doesn't fly at all because you can't depend on the weather.

But in spite of it all, Pangnirtung has been discovered by the tourists. More than 300, mostly Americans and Japanese, make the trip every year to explore the rugged mountains of Auyuittuq National Park, whose peaks are as hard to climb as its name is to pronounce. (If you go, say eye-you-EE-tuck and the natives will be mightily impressed!) The result is that Pangnirtung has its own luxury hotel. Well, maybe luxury isn't quite the word, but it does have clean beds and heat and the bathroom down the hall has hot water. It even has a television set in the lobby so its American guests don't get too homesick. And it has a host-proprietor who's lived in the Arctic for more than 30 years and has a way of making his guests love the place almost as much as he does.

The Arctic has television, hot water, schools, churches and hospitals. It has Mountie posts and Hudson's Bay Company stores. It has Eskimos, too, but no one calls them that any more. There are more than 24,000 of them living in the Northwest Territories trying to hold on to the traditions of their ancestors and hold back the new ways the white man is offering them.

The first white men to encounter Eskimos were part of Martin Frobisher's 1576 expedition to find the Northwest Passage, and they found the natives as hostile as the land. The relationship was conducted at arm's length for the next 350 years until the Canadian Government decided in the 1950s that the Yukon and Northwest Territories were Canadian colonies. With that came dreams of exploiting the natural resources of those territories and the Eskimo and Indian "problem" came to the surface again.

A big part of the problem was that name. White men had called them "Eskimo," from the word in their own language that means "eaters of raw meat." Not a very flattering name, but flattery wasn't what the explorers had in mind anyway. These days, they prefer that the world calls them what they have always called themselves: Inuit. The word in their native language means "the people." The 9,500 Indians who live in the Northwest Territories also call themselves "the people." Their word for it is Dene.

It probably was inevitable that change would come to their world. No one knows for sure, but it's been estimated that the Northwest Territories is very rich in gold and silver as well as tungsten and lead, not to mention uranium, oil and natural gas. There are enough potential riches there to make just about anyone willing to endure two years or so at a "hardship" post up north.

But, of course, civilization being what it is, the men and women who sign up for the "hardship" do everything in their power to make it less hard. They form little communities to make survival easier and they connect them with roads. They build airstrips and they communicate with each other and with the folks back home by satellite. And whatever they do, they do it fast.

The Inuit people, on the other hand, have a different way of coping with life. It's a way that's worked for thousands of years, and not many of them have ever given much thought to the idea that living in the Arctic might constitute some kind of "hardship."

By tradition, they're a nomadic people with a deep love of the land. The father is the centerpiece of the family, not only as a provider-hunter, but as a teacher of his children, and the family is the centerpiece of the Inuit society. Over the generations, they've learned that patience is the only virtue that makes life in the North possible and, as a race, the Inuit are possibly the gentlest people on earth.

But, of course, none of that squares with other people's ideas of "civilized" behavior.

One of the first steps toward bringing the Inuit into step with the rest of us was to stop their nomadic behavior and get them into more formal communities. The move was hailed as humanitarianism at its best. Now these poor people would have access to things their grandparents had never even heard of: good medical care, permanent homes, schools, radio and television, junk food and alcohol. The children were sent off to school, usually hundreds of miles further south. The women were shown food stores, and the men suddenly found themselves with

nothing to do. The family wasn't dependent on hunting skills, there were no children to teach and, besides, the white men had also brought hunting regulations that carried stiff penalties for killing certain animals "out of season." They brought conservation rules that made it an offense to gather wild birds' eggs and told the Inuit men that they should spend their time learning to work for wages like everyone else so they could buy chicken's eggs at the local store for $2.75 a dozen.

While their families are falling apart in the Arctic, the young people are away from home about 10 months a year learning how to cope with a modern world. They also learn English and often forget their own language as well as the traditions of their people. When and if they go back to the Arctic, they don't have much of an idea of how to cope with that world. It's a problem that's driven many of their fathers to drink. And *that's* a problem.

If the old Inuit traditions ever completely vanish, one the whole world will miss is their unique way of carving animals in stone. Up in Frobisher Bay a small group of old men, none of whom has the slightest idea of how old he is, but all of whom are well over 80, eke out a small living by making carvings for sale.

They carve the birds and seals, dogs and bears that once shared their life in the wilderness. "It's hard to describe the pleasure," said one of them. "You see, I hunted all these animals for many years. I came to know them well. We lived together on the land. And from seeing all before, I know how to carve them."

When he was a young man, the caribou was the mainstay of survival. Many families followed a tradition of spending the winter and summer near the coast and moving inland in late summer and fall to stalk the migrating caribou. They used the animal's hide for clothing and tents, its meat for food both for themselves and their dogs, its oil for lighting and for cooking and its bone for tools and weapons. When the white man came, demand for caribou went up and, like the buffalo, herds began coming back north in the spring a little smaller than they had been when they left in the fall. There was a surge in demand for furs and trappers needed more dogs to cover more trap lines. It's been estimated that an Inuit family of four needed about 100 caribou a year to survive in the 19th Century. A team of six sled dogs needed another 50. The result was that the caribou became an endangered species early in this century, and along with them, so did the Inuit.

"I still have trouble with caribou," says Alivukuk, the stone carver in Frobisher Bay. "The legs are difficult unless they are lying down." Why bother carving a standing animal?, you might ask. The old ones would tell you they have no choice about what they carve. They spend hours studying a piece of raw stone before they begin their work. There is a spirit trapped inside, they say, and their function is to liberate it.

The liberation process is often not much more than a few scratches to suggest detail, but the detail is always perceptible, often mystical and strangely striking.

"Eskimo art" has become something highly-prized in warmer parts of Canada, and where there's a market there are always people to satisfy it. But in catering to the more sophisticated tastes of their customers, the younger carvers these days are turning out highly-polished, detailed imitations of the work of their ancestors.

The real thing still lives, though, in the memories of the old-timers whose leathery hands still shape the birds and fish and people they grew up with. As long as their eyes hold out, that part of the Inuit culture is still thriving. But the outside world is very much with them, and their world will never be the same again.

Life for the Indians in the Northwest Territories has changed dramatically, too. They've lived in the North Woods for centuries, having been driven there, according to tradition, by more warlike tribes to the south. They almost never ventured north of the tree line into the land of the Inuit, but their wanderings took them to all parts of the wooded sections, hunting and trapping and surviving.

These days, according to a missionary who has lived among them for two decades on the shore of Great Slave Lake not far from Yellowknife, "young people don't want to go fur-trapping any more because they don't have oranges and TV out in the bush."

What many of them do have is something their grandfathers didn't have: a steady job and a paycheck. Like the Inuit, the Indians in the Northwest Territories are experiencing the mixed blessings of civilization. Over the last few decades, the Government has introduced modern health care in a program that has, among other things, sharply reduced infant mortality. A wonderful thing, to be sure, but that has made Indian families bigger and that puts more pressure on them to increase their income. At the other end of the scale, the new programs have dramatically increased life expectancy. That puts pressure on young families, bound by tradition to take care of the elderly.

The children are sent to schools now and don't learn the

ways of the world from their fathers any more. And if that's not enough strain on family life, they have television and snowmobiles and pickup trucks and houses that need to be heated with increasingly-expensive fuel oil.

Some still live off the land in the traditional ways, but one of their leaders sums up their problems by pointing out that the new ways are chipping away at the old idea of tribes living together and sharing all that they had. In the 1980s, he says, "one man can still live off the land, but a family can't make a living that way. There's a difference."

But if civilization is invading the far North, anyone moving there from the South will tell you it's civilization with a big difference. The manager of the Hudson's Bay store at the northern end of Great Slave Lake is one of them. "It's tough," he says, "but I don't think I could survive any place else. I couldn't live down South any more." His store is the heart of the little town. It's a place for socializing as well as the source of the necessities of life. As the only store in town, it sets the style for the whole area, which makes the manager a very important person in the community. It's a huge responsibility.

He buys furs from the Indians, who most often use the proceeds to pay their bills at the store. And he has to anticipate what his customers will need months before they need it. The nearest warehouse that serves the store is 900 miles away by a dirt road.

Not all the towns in the North are that conveniently accessible. In the mid-1950s the Government established a whole new town along the Mackenzie River well above the Arctic Circle. They called it Inuvik, meaning "place of man," a name some new students of the English language may regard as sexist. But it should be noted that Inuvik, planned with all the facilities of a normal Canadian town, has as its mayor a woman who migrated there from New England almost 20 years ago. When she went there, the town wasn't connected with the rest of Canada by any year-round road; a situation that wasn't corrected until very recently when the Dempster Highway made it possible to drive all the way down to Dawson in the Yukon Territory.

But, right from the beginning, Inuvik had telephones with dials on them, full-time medical care, ice cube machines, television and a well-stocked public library. The library is a busy place during the eight-month winter, when the sun doesn't rise for weeks at a time and the temperature doesn't often get above 30 below zero.

When summer finally comes, it brings hordes of mosquitoes along with it. It also brings tourists, drawn there by the promise of the midnight sun and the incredible beauty of the Arctic. Some of them fall in love with the place and stay, but the population of the town is a fairly constant 3,000 because the traditional pattern in the North is for residents to move out after three or four years. "There isn't much to do here," says one who qualifies as a "native." "Not much, that is, unless you're an outdoorsman and you don't mind mosquitoes and like very long winters."

On the other hand, a lot of people consider it a very good way of life. As Inuvik's mayor describes it, "There is something special about the North. Maybe it's that frontier feeling people have of being kinder to each other out of necessity. You're glad to see someone no matter who it is."

You naturally expect to find wild country in places called the Northwest Territories or the Yukon Territory. But the Province of Quebec, so cosmopolitan in Montreal and Quebec City, doesn't take a back seat to either of them in terms of untamed wilderness. One of the busiest settlements in Northern Quebec is actually a construction site, one of the most ambitious and toughest ever attempted.

It's the James Bay hydroelectric project, some of which is completed and providing electric power for cities as far south as New York. There's more to come and the whole project isn't scheduled to be finished until the late 1980s. In the meantime, thousands of construction workers live in little communities that will become permanent some day, but for now don't even have names. The men and women who live and work there now are commuters from their regular homes about a thousand miles further south. They stay on the job for two-month stretches and then go home for 12 days at company expense. While they're on the job, room and board is free and they have television, movies, even a discotheque to while away the off-hours. The pay is good, too, which is one reason why, when this project is finished, the same workers will probably move on to another similar one. "You get used to this life," says one, "after a while it gets to be the only way." To which one of the women working in the office complex adds, "You'll never see it anywhere else. We've got our own private frontier right here. Some of these guys love to live out of a tent in the middle of nowhere."

Even before the James Bay project, Quebec accounted for nearly half the total hydroelectric output of all of Canada. James Bay will add more than 10,000 megawatts. It's a big business in anybody's terms. But even bigger, for now, is the pulp and paper business, the largest single creator of wealth in Canada, and that was centered in Quebec for many years, too.

The first groundwood pulp mill in Canada was built in Valleyfield, south of Montreal, in the 1860s, and by the turn of the century Canadian mills were producing about a million tons of woodpulp a year. Most of it is made into newsprint, and it's true even today that most Americans wouldn't have the slightest idea what was going on in the world without paper produced in Canada.

After Louis Riel was hanged in the 1880s, the French Canadiens in Quebec decided that it wouldn't be healthy for them to get aboard the bandwagon headed West. But they were touched by the same wanderlust as anyone else at the time, and some moved away from Canada into the New England area. Others, though, went West and North into other parts of Quebec where they found huge stands of virgin forest. The grandfathers of many of them had been lumbermen back in Eastern Canada, but the forests back there had long since been used up. A lot of them went back into the business. Paper mills were good customers for types and sizes of trees that didn't make good lumber, and it didn't take long for the Canadien immigrants to take advantage of a good thing, and eventually the industry moved westward into Ontario and finally as far west as British Columbia.

But not all the Canadiens were French.

The original "habitants" came from Normandy. Today's Quebecker is a new race, even though some three-quarters of them can trace their ancestry directly back to Old France. Any French tourist who visits Quebec City or Montreal notices it right away, and so do the Canadiens. Even the language isn't quite the same. In Quebec, the accent is called Joual, from the French word Cheval, "horse." One of the buggy drivers in Quebec City, who says he'd rather die than give a native Frenchman a tour of his city, says his cousins from Europe are generally loud and, interestingly, difficult to understand. There are some native Frenchmen who have migrated to Canada in recent years, but relatively few. One of them who left home to find a new life finds New France more than just new. Back home, he says, there are social classes and very little communication from one to another. In Quebec, everybody communicates. A little too much, some people will tell you. In the end, though, it creates a more relaxed, open atmosphere and anyone can talk to anyone else without going through the Old World channels of courtesy and false respect. The French immigrant finds that refreshing, the French tourist finds it a little surprising.

Part of the difference comes from the fact that though three-quarters of all Quebeckers call themselves Canadiens and prefer to communicate in French, there are

Germans and Ukranians, Italians and Englishmen mixed into their population. And there are the Irish. In the 19th century, the common religion resulted in some intermarrying between French and Irish immigrants, and even today it isn't uncommon to find homes where both English and French are spoken interchangeably, the children usually speaking their mother's language and the husband and wife each speaking a different language. It's a situation that can cause some interesting family arguments.

The Irish led the movement into the wooded North and the talents they brought from home have served them in good stead as woodcutters and carpenters. And Saint Patrick's Day is a reason for celebration in parts of Quebec almost as much as in Boston.

Religion, specifically the Roman Catholic religion, is at the heart of life in Quebec. With the possible exception of Spain and Ireland and the southern part of Italy, no other place in the world takes Catholicism quite as seriously as Quebec does. The tradition goes back to the French missionaries who stayed behind when the French businessmen went home to a more comfortable life after it became clear that they weren't going to dominate the commercial life of North America.

One of the landmarks of their faith is the Shrine of St. Anne de Beaupré, not far from Quebec City. Its name means "beautiful meadow." A shrine was established on the spot in 1676 by three sailors in thanksgiving for being the only survivors of a shipwreck. In the years since, miraculous cures attributed to Saint Anne have attracted millions of pilgrims there, making it the New World's answer to Lourdes. On July 26, the Feast of Saint Anne, thousands appear to participate in a spectacular candlelight procession through the Stations of the Cross. Many are forced to move slowly on crutches, which they hope to leave behind them with hundreds of others as a testament to cures brought about through the intercession of the mother of the Virgin.

The basilica, which contains a carefully-executed copy of the Scala Santa in Rome, was finished in 1934. Counting a temporary structure that served during the dozen years it took to build it, the present building is the sixth shrine on the same spot and it contains artifacts from each of the others, including a golden statue of the Patroness of the Province that miraculously survived a fire which destroyed the shrine in 1922. One of the Redemptionist Fathers associated with the parish who remembers the fire says, "We lost a mountain of crutches, but the sacred relics were only slightly scorched and the golden statue was not touched though it stood between the steeples."

The basilica is not one of the world's most notable examples of church architecture, but it is among the world's biggest, big enough to hold more than 3,000 worshippers. And the 18th century art and silverwork is among the most impressive in all of North America. The treasures include a chasuble made by Anne d'Autriche in thanksgiving for the birth of a son, who became Louis XIV. The priest points out that traditional Gothic architecture which characterizes the great cathedrals of Europe isn't too practical for the cold climate of Quebec and the architects of this building adapted a Romanesque style more suitable to the Canadian winter.

The husband of Saint Anne is known to the French as Joachim, and the village of St. Joachim, a few miles down the river, is the site of the first art school established in North America. The Bishop of Quebec founded it in 1675 to train woodcarvers and silversmiths to adorn his new churches. Their work appears all over Quebec. But not all their work is limited to representations of saints. In the days of sailing ships, some of the best were built along the St. Lawrence River and the figureheads on their bows provided a different sort of challenge for the woodcarvers trained at St. Joachim. And many of them supplemented their incomes by carving figures of Indians to stand in front of cigar stores all over the continent.

The Bishop who founded the school established his headquarters in Quebec City, and the French Catholic Church is still very much in charge there. The Church's presence there gave the French Canadians a rock to cling to as important as Cape Diamond, the 350-foot rock that impressed Jacques Cartier when he first found it in 1535.

The Indians, who had a little village there, called it Kebec, "the place where the water narrows." Cartier got the message. The narrowing of the river and the height of the rock would make it a perfect place to establish a fortress. He never got around to it, though, and it wasn't until 1608 that Samuel de Champlain replaced the Indian village with a trading post that became the first permanent French settlement in North America.

The English, who were establishing colonies of their own further south, knew a good thing when they saw it and for the next hundred years they made their desires known through repeated attacks on the rock. They even succeeded in gaining control a couple of times, but they never quite succeeded in making it stick. Finally, in 1759, the British General James Wolfe defeated the French General Marquis de Montcalm on the Plains of Abraham just outside the city and Quebec became English territory once and for all. Or so the English thought. According to legend, as General Montcalm was being carried into the city to die, one of his soldiers looked back over his shoulder and shouted to the British, "Je me souviens" "I remember." It's the slogan, a battle cry these days, of the Province of Quebec.

For all their remembering, though, the Quebecois choose to forget that Wolfe, who also died in the battle, was the winning general. Until the early 1960s there was a wooden statue of James Wolfe on the facade of a building in the Old City. It isn't there now because someone threatened to blow the building up if it wasn't removed. It was taken down with great ceremony and moved to a museum in the Citadel, the fortress that is the only building in the city that can truly be called "British." Out on the Plain there are statues of each of the generals, but the plaque that identified Wolfe as the winner was unceremoniously removed some years ago.

It's a city that refused to change anything but a detail of history, and the world should be grateful for that. Quebec City is possibly the most beautiful city on the North American continent and one of the five or six most beautiful cities in the world.

Like so many of the world's cities, there have been attempts to modernize Quebec City over the years and the old buildings were sometimes altered, their stonework covered over, their woodwork painted. But in the 1960s, the Government stepped in and declared the Old City a special zone and went to work restoring it. The city walls, the only such walls in the New World, were first to be spruced up, and in the years since they've separated the historic city from the more modern Quebec City beyond, with its convention center, its underground shopping mall and its Hilton Hotel.

But, inside, the streets are narrow and paved with cobblestones, and most of the buildings are restored to their original condition and house museums and galleries, shops and restaurants. At the heart of it is Place Royale, a small square dominated by a bust of Louis XIV and surrounded by 17th and 18th century buildings. It's known as the birthplace of French civilization in Canada, and it's a place where civilization comes close to experiencing its finest hour.

Like most great cities, Quebec City is a paradise for strollers and there's something to take your breath away at every turn. Moving up from Place Royale to the Upper Town, which can be done by elevator so you don't get too breathless, the reward is the wonderful Chateau Frontenac. Its view of the river was meant to impress you,

but just when you think you've seen it all, La Promenade des Gouverneurs takes you along to the Plains of Abraham and gives even better views of the river on the way.

Beyond, the Parliament Buildings let you know you're still in New France with their French Renaissance magnificence. And nearby there's a reminder of the New World, the highest building in town, a Government office building with a name – Complex G – as memorable as its architecture.

Though it has a few modern buildings, no one would ever accuse Quebec City of having gone "modern." Quebeckers are content to leave that to the Province's other big city, Montreal.

And why not? Montreal is 34 years newer than Quebec City. It was established as a mission in 1642 by Paul de Chomedey, Sieur de Maisonneuve, who called it Ville-Marie de Montreal in honor of the Virgin. He got the name Montreal from Jacques Cartier, who stopped there on the same 1535 voyage that took him to Cape Diamond further up the river. In this case he was impressed by a mountain peak he thought was surely fit for a king and worthy of the name Mont Royal. In his enthusiasm, he named the island in the middle of the river there in honor of his wife, Helene, and that's where Maisonneuve set up his mission some years later.

It's the second biggest city in Canada today, after Toronto, but it hasn't stopped growing yet. People who live there are proud to point out that it's the second largest French-speaking city in the world and that it won't stop growing until it's bigger than Paris and becomes the largest.

If Quebec City is Old World, Montreal is most decidedly new. It's more like Chicago than like Paris. It has an Old Quarter, to be sure, with narrow streets and horse-drawn carriages. It has a cobblestoned square, too, with restored buildings and side-walk cafes. But there's a jarring note there, as well. There's a statue in the center of it honoring the English Admiral, Horatio Nelson. It's a bit of an affront to the French, and there is strong pressure to have it removed and replaced. Fortunately, Montreal once had a mayor named Wilfred Nelson who happened to be French, so Montrealers who make dates to be met near the Nelson statue probably won't have to worry about being stood up no matter whose statue stands in Place Jacques Cartier.

Separatism is as big an issue in Montreal as anywhere in Quebec, but it's not an all-consuming passion. About a third of the people who live there aren't French at all. The city has a growing Chinese quarter and there are more Jews in Montreal than anywhere else in Canada. It's populated by Poles and Lithuanians, Italians and Greeks and a lot of Anglo-Saxons. But it's still two-thirds French and if English is sometimes spoken there, Montreal is as French as any city in the world.

The mix makes it a cosmopolitan place, a center of education and culture, of business and prosperity. It's a city on the move, and Montrealers move from place to place in Le Metro, a subway system that's the envy of every other city in the world. Built in the 1960s, Montreal's subway is clean, of course, it's in Canada after all, but it's also quiet. The trains glide along on rubber tires. There are 45 stations in the system and no two are alike. Each is decorated with tile work and sculpture executed by Montreal artists.

There's a lot more than a great subway system under the streets of Montreal, though. There are six underground shopping and strolling complexes connected to each other by stops on Le Metro. Each of them, in turn, is connected to hotels and office buildings with underground entrances. It's possible for a visitor to spend an entire visit in the city and be completely satisfied by the experience without ever going outdoors. But to do that would be to miss some of the best parts.

One of the very best parts is the park on Mount Royal, the 764-foot mountain that so impressed Cartier and continues to have an effect on everyone who sees Montreal for the first time. The park was designed by Frederick Law Olmstead, who earned near-immortality when he built Central Park in New York. Even if he had never done anything for New York he'd be famous for Mount Royal Park. It started with a wonderful view of the city, but his improvements made it a lot more than a place to look out from.

Montrealers appreciate what he did for them and use the park in summer for afternoon strolls and in winter for ice skating and skiing. The more romantic among them take advantage of the horse-drawn sleighs for a cozy outdoor experience when it's cold, and in spring when other young men's fancy turns to such things, the same horses accomodate them by pulling carriages through the park.

As in any other city, a beautiful park has a good effect on real estate values and one of the best residential neighborhoods in town has always been Westmount on Mount Royal's twin peak. It's a collection of elegant mansions built on the side of the mountain. Until very recently, it was always exclusively English-speaking, a subtle reminder to the French majority where the real

"power" was. The barriers have been moved a bit now, but it still takes money to make it to the hill.

On the other hand, the French-speaking Montrealers of the 19th century had their own exclusive community on the mountain, and anyone who has ever lived there will tell you it's a much pleasanter place to live anyway. Outremont is a little village of old farmhouses tucked among big mansions in a beautiful natural setting. It's near enough to town to be convenient, but light years away from the feeling of being part of a bustling city.

During the height of the summer tourist season, the bustle of the city moves out to Westmount's north slope because the number one attraction for a huge number of visitors is St. Joseph's Oratory, a mountainside basilica dedicated to Canada's patron saint. The monk who built it is said to have been granted special healing powers as a reward for his labors, and about two million people visit his tomb in the church every year because of it.

The Université de Montréal, one of the world's great French-speaking universities, has its campus nearby on the side of the mountain, adding another dash of youth and enthusiasm to the scene.

If Champlain thought the twin-peaked mountain was impressive as nature created it, almost no one can be unimpressed by the things other men have done to make it more attractive. It's an interesting mixture of neighborhoods and landmarks that would make it a very pleasant place to be even if it didn't have such a great view of a great city.

Even though modern transportation makes climbing the mountain a simple thing, it's possible to get sweeping city views without going to the trouble. There are two very good rooftop restaurants in Montreal, one on top of an office building, the other on the top floor of a luxury hotel. Like the view from Mount Royal, it's possible to look down into the United States from up there, to the mountains of New England and New York.

Why build high-rise restaurants in a city with a natural lookout point? Montrealers seem anxious to fill just about any empty space with a restaurant, and once having done that, they set out to make it the best in town. No one can say for sure exactly how many restaurants are scattered over the city, but the number would be in the thousands, and hundreds of them could each easily qualify as the very best in a lesser city.

The accent, naturally, is French, and no city in North

America, New Orleans included, has better French cuisine than Montreal. But the French-Canadians have added touches of their own in many cases that even the *Guide Michelin* might be forced to admit are actually improvements. Even if they didn't, they'd have to admit that the genuine article is as good as in their multi-starred restaurants back in the Old Country.

More like France and much less like any other city in North America, what goes on in the kitchen is much more important in Montreal than what a restaurant dining room looks like; Montrealers never give a place any points for so-called "ambience," which is all too often all that matters in other cities that think of themselves as sophisticated. But in spite of that, some of the best restaurants in town are housed in old buildings that give their dining rooms a very special character, indeed. One has its bar located in a room that was once a secret place for hiding furs, and is reached through a hidden tunnel. Others are in restored town houses, one serves steaks in a converted stable, another is a painstakingly reconstructed Paris bistro.

And after all that good food, what do Montrealers do for exercise? Naturally, there's a good deal of jogging and tennis-playing, skiing and skating going on all over the city these days. But Montreal is a great city for spectator sports, too. Back in 1976, Montreal was the site of the Summer Olympic Games, and the park that was created for them has become one of the centers of life in the city. It's a place to watch tennis matches or bicycle races, or for young adventurers to rent a bike themselves and try whizzing around the banked redwood track. The swimming pool is one of the best in the world and when it's not in use for swimming meets or classes, it's open to the public 12 months of the year.

Olympic Stadium is home to the Montreal Expos, a National League baseball team that just might some day take baseball's World Series out of the United States and into the world. It would be chilly there in October, but worth it! After baseball, professional football takes over and the Montreal Alouettes take on all comers from the Canadian Football League at Olympic Stadium.

In the dead of winter, the Montreal sports scene is far from dead. When the Montreal Canadians are playing hockey at the Forum, almost no one in town can avoid getting deeply involved. Between games, the fans do some fancy skating of their own in all parts of the city, not to mention cross-country skiing on 10 different trails, snowshoeing, Alpine skiing and tobogganing, *all* within the city limits!

Montreal is more than a thousand miles inland from the Atlantic Ocean, but only Vancouver handles more of Canada's seagoing export-import traffic. Credit for that goes to the St. Lawrence Seaway, a system of locks and channels that bypasses waterfalls and rapids and makes the St. Lawrence River a practical connection between the Great Lakes and the Ocean.

The project was open for business in 1959 after the Canadian Government financed the construction of five locks and the American Government built two more to connect Montreal with Lake Ontario.

Lake Ontario, in turn, is connected to Lake Erie by the Welland Ship Canal, a 28-mile ditch that bypasses Niagara Falls and allows ships to get all the way to Detroit from the Atlantic. But the Seaway doesn't end there. It's possible for ocean-going ships to make their way all the way to the middle of Ontario at the head of Lake Superior, and a great many of them do, as long as the channels aren't frozen over.

The Seaway between Montreal and the ocean is kept open year-round by ice-breakers. All year round, dredgers keep the thousand-mile channel at a depth of about 35 feet. The overall length of the Seaway, from the Atlantic to Duluth, Minnesota, is 2,300 miles, roughly the same distance, as the seagull flies, from the coast of Newfoundland to the coast of England. But more impressive than that is the fact that as ships move inland, they also go from sea level to a height of 602 feet above it. It's accomplished by a series of more than 16 locks, half of them in the 28-mile stretch of the Welland Canal.

Less than 10 years after the Seaway was opened, Montreal showed the world that it had become one of the world's most important cities by mounting a World's Fair called EXPO 67. The occasion was the hundredth anniversary of Canadian Confederation, and if all Canada did, indeed, get in on the act, it was a showcase for Quebec's future as much as anything else. The show took place on the islands in the river, including some new ones made especially for the occasion. Many of them are still part of the city's parks system. Like all International Expositions, EXPO 67 was an occasion to trot out the new ideas of new architects, and the pavilions they created, though puzzling to some, have inspired building all over Canada in almost the same way the Canadian Pacific hotels set the architectural style a half-century ago.

But the style of most World's Fairs is to pass their style along, never to make themselves a permanent example of it. It's another thing that makes Montreal different. EXPO 67 is still there and still attracting millions of visitors every year.

They call it "Man and His World" these days, reflecting the original theme of the Fair. Some of the sections of the original were replaced by facilities for the Olympics, but what's left of EXPO is enough to keep both Montrealers and their visitors occupied, happy and well-fed through summer evenings. It provides them with adventure, too, at La Ronde, an amusement park that takes up more than 35 acres with death-defying rides, games and exotic restaurants.

There's a military museum and an aquarium on one of the islands too, for people who get their thrills in different ways, and a key attraction at the museum is drills performed alternately by a French Colonial company and a Scottish company. Each appears in the colorful costumes of their predecessors, the only difference being that they don't fight with each other. Not in public, anyway.

It gets quiet out in the river in winter when most of the rides and restaurants are shut down for the season. But there are other good things to occupy the Montrealer's mind during the cold months. The city is within easy striking distance of what may be the absolute best ski country in the entire world, an amazing range of mountains called the Laurentians.

It's not a range of spectacular, rugged peaks like the Alps or the Rockies. One of the most popular Laurentian peaks, Mount Tremblant, is puny by comparison even to mountains further north in Quebec. But there are more ski resorts in the Laurentians than any other mountain range anywhere, and all of them are better than average. One reason is the amount of snow that falls there. Even in a drought year, some 150 inches of snow are sure to fall on the Laurentian slopes. And that famous, cold Canadian air guarantees a season that begins early in November and continues until the middle of May.

Skiing hasn't always been the popular attraction it is today, and it might still be just a spectator sport without the Laurentian courses, many of which were laid out 50 years ago. The first of them, at Shawbridge, opened in 1928 by a skier with the wonderful name of Jack Rabbit Johanssen, showed the Canadian man in the street the joys of a skiing weekend. The Lodge at Mount Tremblant, with access to more than a dozen ski areas with some 35 miles of trails, attracted the pre-war version of the Jet Set, and by the mid-'40s, people looking for winter vacations began heading north instead of south.

The mountains, probably the oldest in North America, were molded to their present gentleness thousands of years ago by the great glaciers. But they aren't so gentle that they didn't form a natural barrier to the original settlers of Canada. When the urge to move on hit them, the first Canadians usually stopped when they saw mountain peaks ahead. But the animals they displaced when they built their towns and cities along the St. Lawrence weren't so fussy and headed for the hills. Their descendants are still there, living in protected game preserves and national parks. Man has followed them by now, of course, but the invasion has been gentle, and the communities in the mountains are most often charming little villages with French names and French accents. The hills are dotted with hotels and resorts, too, but in spite of the fact that their season is a year-round thing, very few of them could be called "commercial," even by the most discriminating traveller.

In summer, the Laurentians are an oasis from civilization, with beautiful lakes and rivers, abundant wildlife, clean air. It's a place for camping and canoeing, hunting and fishing, for getting back in touch with what makes life itself a genuine pleasure.

But to many people, the Laurentians are at their very best in the fall. New Englanders are quick to tell anyone that their fall foliage is the most spectacular, the most beautiful anywhere in the world. There's no denying that the New England autumn is a joy to behold, but Canadians know it's only a reflection of the spectacle nature provides for them in the Laurentians.

Hunting and fishing and even camping are strictly controlled by regulations designed to protect the area and the living things within it, which gives the children of today's visitors an assurance that they, too, will have the same advantages of a natural retreat within easy distance of thriving cities.

Thriving cities go right up to the edge of the Laurentians, including one of Canada's major industrial cities, Trois Rivières. It has the distinction of having become Canada's first industrial center after the Forges de Saint-Maurice was established there in 1729. Its principal product in the 18th and 19th Centuries was the famous Rabaska canoe, a 40-foot long birch bark boat that took its name from the Athabaska River in Western Canada. It was the boat that won the West and a great many of the men who paddled Rabaskas through the wilderness were born in Trois Rivières.

Although it has been settled since 1615, when Champlain set up a trading post at the mouth of the Saint-Maurice River, Trois Rivières never got around to formally declaring itself a city until 1963. The Saint-Maurice Valley is like that. The people there like a rural atmosphere, and even though the city is the place where Great Lakes grain ships transfer their cargo to ocean-going vessels and the Valley produces more than one hundred million pulpwood logs a year for the biggest paper mills in the world, the pace is relaxed, the forests quiet, the farms orderly and well-maintained. Many of the farms also double as tourist attractions, as do farms all over Quebec. Family groups are welcome as paying guests in farmhouses registered with the Department of Agriculture, and a great many of them return year after year just for the food.

The area connects with the Laurentians through two huge parks: the De la Mauricie National Park, 200 square miles of wilderness dotted with more than 60 lakes and more rivers than anyone cares to count; and Saint-Maurice Park, 617 square miles of territory that was once the private preserve of hunting and fishing clubs. "Wildly beautiful" is the way the official tourist office describes the parks, and, just as official Quebec has made no attempt to "improve" on nature, there is no way to improve the description.

As if anyone needed any more elbow room, the Government created a third park, Mastigouche, in 1971. Its 678 square miles border the other two, forming a natural preserve bigger than Rhode Island. It's a place trout fishermen dream about.

Quebec has another type of finny creature that isn't hunted any more, but still provides a sense of adventure for people who go to the trouble to look for it. There are whales in the St. Lawrence River.

There are whales in a lot of parts of the world, of course. In fact, one that was once tagged off the Novia Scotia coast turned up seven years later in Spain. But the best place to watch for whales is at the mouth of the St. Lawrence in late summer and early fall. Old-timers in Quebec say that the creatures are coming in increasing numbers these days because they're basically friendly and like to look back at the boatloads of whale-watchers who have come to look at them. A more important reason may be that it has been illegal to hunt whales in Eastern Canada since 1972. But the best reason of all is that there is an abundant food supply for them in the Gulf of St. Lawrence, and these animals, which often weigh as much as 100 tons, need to consume about 5 percent of their body weight a day just to survive.

Whale-watching began in earnest in 1970, when the Montreal Zoological Society organized an excursion down the river for its members. It must have been an idea whose time had come because they've been doing it ever since, scheduling three trips a year that include two days on the water in the company of a whale expert. The Museum of Natural Sciences in Ottawa offers a similar excursion, and in the years since the first trip, independent operators have got in on the act, including some who offer trips from Massachusetts.

There are some 20 species of whale in the North Atlantic, including the Right Whale, which was the favourite of the 19th Century whalers who gave them the name because they were the "right" ones to kill. What made them right was that they had more oil than other species, and therefore more profit potential, and the oil made them buoyant after a kill, making the whaler's job a whole lot easier.

Whales are mammals, not fish, and have to come to the surface once in a while to get a breath of fresh air. Their nostrils are on the top of their heads, and before taking air into them, they first exhale the water they have accumulated along with their food. The result is a spectacular waterspout that can sometimes be seen for miles. It was a dead giveaway of their presence for the mighty whale hunters, and it still helps the whale-watchers know where to look. Some whales can stay under the surface for more than two hours, so patience is the number one requirement for people who hope to see them. But the reward is worth it.

The spout is more than a visual event. Hundreds of gallons of water shoot up 20 or 30 feet into the air in a matter of seconds with a rushing sound no one who hears it can ever forget. Then a glistening object arches above the surface growing larger and larger. At first it looks like a log, but quickly grows to become bigger than a house. People on the excursion boats often get so excited they forget to take pictures, and no one looks at a watch to see how long the animal is on the surface. It's never more than a minute or two, though sometimes a whale will resurface several times before going back to the bottom for a bite to eat. But for people who experience the adventure, those few minutes are expanded into hours of excited conversation, first with their fellow whale-watchers, and eventually with the folks back home.

Even if the actual moment of truth on a whale-watching tour may be just a few minutes out of two days, the hours on a small ship are rewarding in themselves, and though some people choose to rough it by sleeping on board, the ship puts in at Rivière du Loup for the two nights of the excursion. The little town, set on terraces rising up from the river into the Notre Dame Mountains, is the gateway to Gaspé, a place that was once a home-away-from-home to Viking adventurers and considered a good place to live by French fishermen in the 17th Century.

Cartier claimed it for the King of France when he visited there in 1534. Nearly 500 Indians stood by as he erected a giant cross to mark it as the King's territory, and when he left they shrugged their shoulders and went about their business. His visit gave them plenty to talk about around their campfires, though. A few years later, Champlain gave them even more to talk about by taking one of their own words to serve as a name for the place. The word "Gespeg," to them, meant "the end of the earth." Why he picked *that* name was as mysterious to them as their new ruler and that wooden thing that had been solemnly placed in their midst.

As far as they were concerned, their peninsula was all there was to the world, and even when Europeans began arriving several years later, it was still a territory removed from outside contact. A road was finally built in 1858, but it was a rocky road and not many people used it. A railroad broke through to the edge of the peninsula in 1876, but it was 40 more years before anyone thought to extend it all the way to the end. And a good road didn't exist until 1929.

The result is that the Gaspé is like a place that time forgot. Even Mother Nature herself seems to have forgotten it in the cycles of change that are forever altering landscapes. Its rugged mountains were largely untouched by the glaciers that softened most of Eastern North America, and some varieties of trees and plants long extinct in other parts of the world still thrive in the Chic-Choc Mountains. There are species of birds there, too, that are almost never seen in other places, and the herds of deer, moose and caribou are as large as they ever were.

In any other place, the Chic-Chocs would be a major tourist attraction, but there's a better one on the Gaspé: the sea. The underwater terraces around the edge of the Peninsula make it a perfect breeding ground for cod, and for generations huge fishing fleets from Europe crossed the ocean just for the season. Some settled down, of course, and when word got around that some of the best salmon in the world were swimming in the Matane River, more Basques, Normans and Bretons followed them. Loyalists who left New England in 1776 were rewarded for their loyalty to the Crown with land grants in the Gaspé. The English King also gave a grant to a group from Guernsey and Jersey that was very much like the Hudson's Bay Company. They set up company stores and established themselves as suppliers of cod, tuna, salmon, lobster and other such delicacies. It wasn't long before they had competition, and together they managed to deplete the marine life to the point that the Government was finally forced to institute strict regulations.

No matter how hard they tried, though, they couldn't take all the marine life out of the gulf, and fishing is still a major industry there. They weren't able to change the area's French accent, either.

English-speaking tourists call the Gaspé's most beautiful spot "Percy," but the natives don't mind as long as their visitors understand that it wasn't named for some English settler, but for the fact that the 300-foot rock, just offshore on the East Coast, has a natural arch that prompted the French settlers to call it Le Rocher Percé.

There were two arches in Percé Rock until the pounding ocean caused one of them to collapse in 1845, but many people think the tower that was left makes the rock all the more interesting. The Rock is near enough to shore to be reached on foot when the tide is out, but the best views of it are from shore, especially at sunrise when the first light reaches the village through the 50-foot hole in the rock. When it's shrouded in fog it looks like a huge ocean liner bearing down on the harbor.

The Rock is home to thousands of gulls and cormorants as well as other sea birds, and it's a favorite visiting place for the birds that live three miles offshore on Bonaventure Island, a Government-controlled bird sanctuary that has the biggest colony, some 50,000-strong, of gannets in North America.

Is it any wonder they call Quebec "La Belle Province?" It's Canada's biggest, much bigger than Texas, slightly bigger than Alaska and more diverse than either of them. Each of Canada's Provinces has its own personality, but none of them has as strong a personality as Quebec. There's a *joie de vivre* there that makes it a pleasure to visit, a fabulous place to live.

Though the oldest European settlement in North America is in Florida, the second and third oldest are St. John's, Newfoundland, and Annapolis Royal in Nova Scotia. St. John's was an English Colony, but the other, established in 1604 as Port Royal, was French and acted as a magnet for French settlers who adapted an Indian word and called the territory Acadie.

It didn't take long for the English from New England to take over and begin a battle with the French that lasted for 150 years. The English King added fuel to the fire by giving a land grant in coastal Canada to his friend Sir William Alexander. The French in North America were calling their colonies "New France," the English had already established "New England," and the Spanish were encouraging adventurers to settle in "New Spain." Alexander, not being a man to buck a trend, called his territory Nova Scotia, "New Scotland." The only problem was that some six thousand Europeans who had settled there called the place Acadia and they talked to each other in French.

Finally, in 1755, when the British felt they had enough power, the Royal Governor announced that the Acadians weren't welcome there any more and packed them off into exile.

The Acadians were an independent lot. Most had originally come from France, but there were a fair number who joined them from Ireland, Scotland and England. Like the Métis in the West, they slowly became an independent race, speaking a language that was French, but not quite the same language spoken in France. In a little more than a century, they were asked to change their allegiance more than a dozen times, mostly switching back and forth between England and France, but once being put under the control of the Dutch. Through it all, though, they never once suffered an identity crisis. They were Acadians, that's all.

They traded with the English in Boston and corresponded with families back in France. The French Government thought it had them in its hip pocket, and the British Government fretted over whether they were as neutral as they claimed. The solution was to scatter them, and in the process families were sometimes broken up.

Some Acadians went back to France, others were shipped off to the English colonies in North America. About a thousand destined for the Virginia Colony were turned away at the border by a Governor who told them they were England's problem and to go to England to live. The English didn't want them either, and eventually shipped them over to France to be reunited with the Acadians already there. The French didn't want them and they themselves didn't particularly want to be in France. Life in North America had changed them. The question was finally settled by settling them on the island of Belle-Ile-en-Mer off the Brittany coast, where their descendants still live, not as Frenchmen but as Acadians.

Another large group of them still lives in exile, tenaciously clinging to the culture of their Canadian ancestors, in the Mississippi delta near New Orleans. Only their name has been changed. In the United States, they call them "Cajuns."

Meanwhile, back in Nova Scotia, the British moved in as soon as the Acadians moved out. Most of the new arrivals were Loyalists from New England. Though they had left

their possessions behind them, they took their slaves along and by the end of the 18th century, there were some 1,500 former slaves living along the Canadian coast. The Government in Halifax had ruled that slavery was illegal in Nova Scotia and then it went a step further with an offer to resettle the Blacks in Africa if they wanted to go. Those who took advantage of the offer eventually went to Africa's West Coast where they established a new nation they called Sierra Leone.

In the next century, of course, more Blacks arrived in Canada via the "underground railroad," a route to freedom from the Southern States established in the years before the American Civil War. Most of them stayed to become Canadians and their descendants live there today.

Some of the Acadians drifted back home again, too, joining their relatives who had avoided deportation by hiding in the woods when the British soldiers came to round them up. But when all is said and done, Nova Scotia is as much "New Scotland" today as it ever has been. Scots began arriving right at the start of the 19th century, and before 1830 the dominant language of Acadia was Gaelic and the sounds in the air, formerly the "murmuring pines and hemlock" described by Longfellow in his epic "Evangeline," were made by bagpipes.

Longfellow's "forest primeval" still exists but Canada's Atlantic Provinces: Nova Scotia, Newfoundland, New Brunswick and Prince Edward Island, are dominated by the sea. They form the point of North America closest to Europe and just about every explorer who set out for the New World found it along this Northern Coast. Leif Ericson was probably first, but the Englishman John Cabot is usually credited with having discovered what he called a "New Founde Isle" in 1497. It was a popular place for fishermen in the years that followed and probably became the world's first international settlement, with men from Spain and Portugal, England and France making it their home away from home when the fishing was good. But international settlements weren't considered a very good idea in the 16th century and in 1583 Sir Humphrey Gilbert officially made it an English colony. That didn't stop the French, though, nor the Spanish, nor the Dutch, all of whom left their mark. Most of them went for the good fishing and all of them insisted on a monopoly. The English, considering themselves in control, decided that the best way to protect their monopoly was to forbid settlement.

That was much easier said that done. One of the English laws made it illegal to build a house with a chimney, which made surviving the winters a bit tricky. For those who did manage, another law was passed forbidding them to establish farms. But even the long arm of the British Empire couldn't penetrate all the coves and inlets along the coast, and many of them became little settlements complete with chimneys and tiny vegetable gardens. Hiding out from the British kept them hidden from the world as well, and even as late as 1949, when Newfoundland officially became part of the Canadian Confederation, many of the little communities could only be reached by boat and few of them had electricity or telephones, not to mention schools or medical care. Just about all of them speak English, but because of their long years of isolation, their accents are from another time and many of the expressions they use are totally incomprehensible to other Canadians. Some other Canadians call them "Newfies," usually in jokes that are less than complimentary. But the Newfoundlers have a phrase it would help those other Canadians to learn:

"Nofty was 40 when he lost the pork," they say. Without a translator, even though the words are English, it would be hard to know that what they mean is that "you can never be sure of anything."

The old Newfie image is changing fast thanks to what Pierre Trudeau called "a revolution between the ears." The clocks in Newfoundland are a half hour ahead of clocks in the rest of North America, and the Province is determined to put itself ahead, too. One of the things that might do it is the huge oil and gas field off its coast. Another is the iron ore and hydroelectric power output of Labrador, which is part of the Province.

In other times, the mainstay of the area was fishing, and it's still a $100,000,000 industry there, but the sea-going processing plants from other countries have skimmed off so much of the cod that most of the one-family operations have been forced out of business, leaving Newfoundland with the biggest unemployment rate in Canada.

That's changing now, but those little villages are still there and they're as charming as ever.

There are times, though, when it isn't possible to find them. Another of the things that makes the Maritime Provinces unique is the fog. Londoners may once have been proud of their pea soup fog, but the Canadian version is much thicker and it swirls around a lot, making navigation even tougher. It's no wonder that foghorns were invented by a New Brunswick musician who noticed that deep bass notes traveled great distances and built a steam-powered bass horn to call the attention of passing ships to the rocks that lined the shore.

All the Maritime Provinces have shorelines out of proportion to their size. Newfoundland, the tenth largest island in the world, boasts 10,900 miles of coast. Prince Edward Island, though a good deal smaller, has 1,000 miles of inlets and bays. New Brunswick's coastline is 1,400 miles long. And sailing the coast of Nova Scotia is a voyage of 4,615 miles.

Naturally, sailing is a way of life in all of them, and in the days of wooden ships and iron men Nova Scotia, all by itself, ranked fourth in the world in the number of registered ships. It was no coincidence that Samuel Cunard, one of the great "English" ship owners, first put out to sea from Halifax, the place where he was born.

There's another surprising side to Nova Scotia. It really looks like Scotland. The image is helped along with place names like New Glasgow and Balmoral Mills and the annual "Gatherings of the Clans" in places like Pugwash, Trenton, Cape Breton and Antigonish. The highland games, punctuated by pipe band tattoos, caber-tossing and Scotch whisky-tasting save a lot of Americans the cost of a trip to Europe.

The accent is more British in New Brunswick, the original home of Lord Beaverbrook, the English newspaper owner, whose name appears all over the Province in theaters, churches and other buildings he funded. But the beauty of New Brunswick is more in its landscape than in its buildings. It's a place of rolling farmland and covered bridges, dense forests, high mountains and deep valleys. Its most spectacular attraction is the Bay of Fundy on the Southeast Coast, which boasts the highest tides in the world, rising and falling as much as 30 feet and in the process creating strange coves and caves and odd rock formations.

In contrast, the shoreline along the Gulf of St. Lawrence, known as the Acadian Coast, is an area of sandy beaches, some of the best in all Canada, washed by the warm waters of the Gulf Stream.

But mostly, New Brunswick is a land of rural countryside, quiet and peaceful; a place they call "Canada's Picture Province."

Prince Edward Island, Canada's smallest Province, is just a 45-minute ferryboat ride away from New Brunswick. It's a place of gentle farmland, too, and its beaches, like the ones across the Northumberland Strait, are quite the best on the East Coast north of Virginia. But what lures half-a-million visitors there every year is the peace and quiet and the incredible way of life of the less than 125,000 people who live there. It's a crescent-shaped island about 140 miles long and, at its narrowest, 4 miles wide, and most of the people live on farms, which they tend in a neat and orderly fashion. The "city folks," about 20,000 of them, live in Charlottetown, the Island's biggest city.

Canadians in every Province are proud to report that theirs is the most independent in the whole Confederation, and the people of P.E.I. are no different. But the islanders back up their claim by pointing out that the first meetings to consider Confederation were held there in 1864 and they themselves didn't join until almost ten years later.

It's always been tough to get Canadians to agree on matters of politics. The problem has been with them from the start, and has shown itself in some peculiar ways. Take, for instance, the question of where to put a central Government if they ever managed to get one together. The first step toward Confederation was the uniting of Upper and Lower Canada in 1841. Even though they couldn't agree on how it should be governed, they decided the new parliament should meet in Kingston and commandeered a hospital to serve as a meeting place. Kingston got its hospital back two years later when the lawmakers moved into a converted market in Montreal. The locals burned the place down in a protest demonstration six years later and the capital was moved to a safer location in Toronto. The Upper Canada parliament buildings were still standing there so there was no housing problem, except for the fact they had been converted into an insane asylum. A great many Canadians at the time thought that was entirely appropriate. The legislators didn't agree, apparently, because a year later they moved on to Quebec. Over the next dozen years they alternated between Toronto and Quebec, regularly picking up and relocating all the machinery of government at great expense and even greater confusion.

Finally, Queen Victoria settled the argument over whether Toronto or Quebec ought to be the permanent capital by ruling that neither of them ought to be. Instead she picked a tough little lumber town that had been called Bytown just a few years before and was still, in the opinion of a lot of politicians, a place to pass by. But by 1857, when the Queen spoke, the town had a new name, and by speaking she gave it a new future. Its name had been changed two years before to Ottawa in honor of the Outaouac Indians who lived nearby.

She made sure her decision would stick by financing the great Gothic Parliament Buildings that are a national treasure today. The Prince of Wales, the future King Edward VII, laid the cornerstone in 1860 and the buildings opened for business in 1865 in plenty of time for the proclamation of Confederation.

Boosters are fond of calling Ottawa "the most Canadian of cities," and if it's possible for there to be such a thing, they're probably right. It's open, clean, friendly and well-planned, and **that's** Canadian. Its museums, galleries and theaters reflect every aspect of Canadian life and culture. Until recent years, the provincial highway system had surrounded all the major cities in the East with tons of concrete, but the roads into the capital from Montreal in the North and from Ontario in the South dwindled down to two-lane affairs as they approached Ottawa. It was a subtle display of provincial authority over federal power – and **that's** Canadian.

The highways from Ottawa into other parts of Ontario lead into what the tourist agencies like to call "the most Canadian of Provinces." Other Canadians call it the most American. There are good arguments to support both causes.

Ontario is big. Ontario's winters are cold. It has an English background and, in parts, a French accent. It's heavily industrial with thriving cities. It has huge farms and it has small towns. It has areas untouched by the hand of man. All of that is very Canadian.

Ontarians have been fighting off American influence right from the beginning, but the influence is there in the business and industrial centers. Even the population itself has an American influence. After the War of 1812, Americans flocked across the border to become Canadians, and Ontario was their prime destination. By 1815, three-fifths of all Ontarians had been born in the United States. But then, as now, the majority of the people living in Ontario trace their roots back to Great Britain and Ontario, especially in the South, which is as British today as any of the cities and towns across the ocean that gave Canada such place names as Cambridge and Woodstock or even London.

The heart of British tradition in Ontario is generally within easy travelling distance of one of North America's most spectacular attractions, Niagara Falls. It's the corner of Canada that's probably visited by more foreign tourists than any other. But, unfortunately for them, too many of them stop at the Falls and don't venture any deeper into Canada. They don't know what they're missing!

Travelers from Europe bound for New York often include Niagara in their itinerary, probably because the American side of the Falls is in New York State. Not realizing that New York City is at one end of the State and Niagara Falls is at the other, they find themselves committed to a 400-mile bus ride as part of their tour. Then when they get there, they find out that the best place to see the Falls is on the Canadian side. By that time, they're either too tired or too short of time to take advantage of the opportunity that's been handed to them, the chance to see more of Canada.

Niagara Falls is its own reward, to be sure, especially at night when colored floodlights add to its incredible beauty. And there's enough to do right there to make the trip worthwhile. But just a few miles away at Niagara-on-the-Lake they could be enjoying a play by George Bernard Shaw in the world-famous Shaw Festival. Not much further from there, they could visit Stratford, on the Avon River, of course, for one of the world's greatest Shakespearian Festivals.

There are festivals all over the place in Southern Ontario. There are antiques festivals, arts festivals, country fairs and highland games. There are colonial restorations surrounded by tobacco fields (yes, tobacco!) and opportunities for wine-tasting in local vineyards. One of Canada's great concert halls is in a Scottish castle near a steelmill in Hamilton. And there are forts and stockades enough to satisfy any history buff.

Tourists from England would be right at home there, especially in the old country inns, many of which are terrific places to stop for tea in late afternoon. The place names are familiar to Englishmen, too, until they come upon a little town called Paris, which could provide a mild culture-shock; even it is English in character. The name doesn't come from the capital of France, nor from the man who caused the Trojan War, but from the fact that the town's major industry once was the mining of gypsum to make plaster-of-Paris. Its other claim to fame, by the way, is that it was on the receiving end of the first long distance phone call ever made. The call was made to no less a person than Alexander Graham Bell, a native Canadian, from his home town in Brantford, just a few miles away.

These days, when Canadians say, "Hello, Central, get me Paris," they usually want to be plugged in to Paris, France, and the lion's share of those calls probably go out from Toronto, the biggest, busiest city in Canada. It wasn't always the case.

When the British singer Lulu did her thing in Toronto a few years ago, she told an interviewer, "I was in Toronto 12 or 15 years ago and it was a real hick town. But now it's simply super!"

One of the things that made it "super!" was its transformation from a basically British outpost to a destination for immigrants from all over the world. In the process it became an international city. When the local government wants to communicate with its constituents, it does so in six different languages with official forms printed in English, French, Spanish, Italian, Greek and Chinese.

As recently as the 1930s, whole sections of Toronto were on a water rationing system that limited their running water to an hour or two a day. There were no sewers, no sidewalks and the electric lights flickered a lot when they worked at all. In the 1950s the city fathers grabbed their collective bootstraps and transformed the place into a city other cities look to for ideas.

One of the changes they made was the creation of the "Toronto Sunday," a day for relaxation and fun. Anybody who lives in any city in the world would smile indulgently at that idea. That's been a custom among city-dwellers since long before the Indians gathered here and gave it their name for "meeting place." But for Toronto, having a good time on Sunday was a symbolic gesture that put it squarely on the side of the future. Less than 30 years ago, the city simply shut down on Sunday. Literally. Stores not only closed their doors, but they also drew special curtains over the windows so no one could idle away the day with window shopping. Churches were open, to be sure, and anything but church-going on a Sunday was illegal, or at the very least frowned upon. Nobody frowns on Sunday in Toronto any more. Probably because they have so much to smile about.

Because it was a late bloomer, Toronto learned from the mistakes of the other great cities of the world. Its public transportation system is one of the world's best, which makes the traffic problem easier to handle. Its zoning laws create a mix that keeps the city vital day and night, and helps keep the young people from longing for life in the suburbs.

That's not to say they're without problems. But Toronto's solutions to its problems have earned it the reputation of being a "People City." When the huge glass dome was being built for Eaton's Centre, the downtown shopping mall that houses the flagship of Eaton's chain of department stores along with some 300 other retailers, a fine old church stood in the way. In any other city, the church might have been saved if enough people complained. But in Toronto they went a step further and altered the plan so that the new Galleria wouldn't block the sun from the church building.

They take building seriously in Toronto. It's only natural for a growing city. But they seem to know the difference between growing big and growing up. Parks and open spaces are as important as tall buildings and Toronto has its share of both, including the tallest free-standing tower in the world and a tree-lined boardwalk that takes strollers along a quiet, sandy beach.

The tallest structure, obviously a landmark, is the CN Tower, which, at 1,815 feet, is about 360 feet higher than the world's tallest building, Chicago's Sears Tower. The top, often covered by clouds, is reached by outside elevators with glass fronts that are an experience in themselves. Near the top, but well below the communications mast and observation deck, is the "sky pod" containing a revolving restaurant that offers diners a view that often includes Niagara Falls, about 80 miles to the south.

At night, part of the observations deck becomes a disco, the highest in the world, of course. It adds another dimension of culture to a city that has its own resident symphony orchestra, an opera company and a ballet company, all of which are among the world's best.

There are galleries and museums all over Toronto, including the Art Gallery of Ontario, proud owner of more than 300 sculptures by Henry Moore, the biggest collection in North America. Most of them were given to the Gallery by Moore himself, who fell in love with Toronto in a strange way.

When plans were announced for a new City Hall in 1957, everyone in town took sides over whether or not it ought to be built along the lines of the original plan. One of the victims of the battle was a Moore sculpture, *The Archer*, slated to be placed in the courtyard. When the city council refused to buy it, a group of citizens began collecting money on their own and eventually raised enough to circumvent the wishes of their elected officials. The sculpture stands there today in Nathan Phillips Square, a much-loved witness to rock concerts, impromptu political debates and budding romances over brown bag lunches.

Toronto is a city any artist could love. From the ultra-modern Royal Bank Plaza with its towers glittering with gold dust and its collection of modern art to the fantastic Casa Loma, a strange medieval-looking castle in the heart of the city, there's enough contrast to stimulate any creative soul.

As the city that accounts for about a fifth of all the manufacturing in Canada and about a third of the country's income, Toronto is clearly one of the most important business centers in the Western Hemisphere. But there's no business like show business, and it's always been known as a good theater town.

Major movies begin their runs in Toronto and, increasingly, many of those major movies have their roots in Canada. Back in the earliest days of movie-making, a young Toronto girl named Gladys Marie Smith had to go to the United States to make her mark. After changing her name to Mary Pickford, she became "America's Sweetheart," but she never let anyone forget that she was Canadian. If she had come along a few years later, she may never have left home.

In 1939, the Canadian Parliament appropriated $250,000 to promote the production of films "in the national interest." The money was used to establish the National Film Board, which took over an old sawmill as its headquarters and began sending locally-produced movies to small Canadian towns to give Canadians their first look at the wonders of their own country and, not incidentally, at some of the wonderful talent in their midst.

Over the years, the Board has pioneered new filmmaking techniques, particularly in the animation field, and has produced more than 30 feature films of its own. Over the years, they've earned an international reputation punctuated by some 2,000 awards, including six Oscars.

From its base in Montreal, the Film Board produces about 100 films a year, ranging from documentaries on famous Canadians like Paul Anka or United States Senator S.I. Hayakawa, to instructions on how to salt codfish. It also maintains film libraries all over Canada, following in the tradition of the early projectionists who roamed the country in the '40s.

Naturally, the Film Board's biggest markets are in Ontario where the most people are, a third of Canada's population, in fact, but outdoor activities are very big in the lives of average Ontarians just as they are all over Canada.

The fact that Ontario is heavily populated and heavily industrial is only relative. Ontario is also big. Toronto's Younge Street leads out of town and then north in a big arc around the top of Lake Superior then on west to Thunder Bay and beyond to Lake of The Woods and the Minnesota border. It's a trip of well over 1,000 miles and though it passes through plenty of towns along the way, it's a trip that offers peace and solitude. And inspiration.

It skirts the forest and lakes and spectacular resorts that have made Ontario a vacation destination for generations, and plunges into wilderness that hasn't changed much since the French trappers ran their lines there and where loggers still work as they always have. It goes through quiet woodlands, past bubbling brooks and roaring waterfalls. It passes game preserves and ski resorts, deep canyons and breathtaking mountain lookouts.

The road passes very near to Algonquin Provincial Park, a 3,000-square-mile wilderness preserve less than 150 miles from Toronto. There are marked routes for canoes on the Pave's rivers and streams that extend for more than 1,000 miles, enough to make anyone's arms tired just thinking about it. There are hiking trails, too, and a modern highway for people who prefer to commune with nature in a less strenuous way. The highway cuts through just a corner of the Park, though, leaving the rest of it clean and quiet, which is what a park ought to be, after all.

North and west of the Park, along the route the great French explorers followed when they went west, is the nickel capital of the world, Sudbury. It's not only the greatest concentration of the metal, but it's the place where it was first discovered by a local blacksmith. Tom Flanagan was his name, and like a lot of people in the area he spent his spare time kicking over rocks looking for a vein of silver or iron ore, anything that might turn his life around. One day he found some glittering stuff he thought might be copper. It turned out it wasn't, but nobody could figure out what it was. Tom said it was "Old Nick's Copper," put there by the Devil to frustrate prospectors. Even before they found out it was tarnish-proof and valuable in alloys, local people shortened Tom's name for it, and nobody has ever thought to call it anything but nickel ever since.

The world's richest silver vein was opened a little north of there in 1903 by another blacksmith who had nothing more in mind than killing a fox. When Fred Larose tossed his hammer at the little animal he missed and hit a rock instead. It was a lucky break for both Fred and the fox because there was enough silver in the rock to make him incredibly rich. It was a great day for the little town of Cobalt, too. Almost overnight it became home to more than 20,000 adventurers, many of whom were lucky enough to strike it rich, too. There was so much silver in Cobalt they even made a shiny sidewalk out of it.

Adventurers who passed Cobalt by and kept going north got even richer mining gold. Except for South Africa, the mines in the Porcupine area have produced more gold than any other in the world. And today, Timmins is the location of the richest silver and zinc mine anywhere.

Young people who look longingly back at those days when a man could become a millionaire overnight don't have to look further than a little town east of Sault Ste. Marie called Elliot Lake. There was no town there at all in 1954, but there were a lot of little wooden stakes all over the countryside.

They marked prospectors' claims in a hundred-thousand acre uranium field. The game may be played by different rules these days, but opportunities are still there.

Canada is as much a land of opportunity as it ever has been, especially in the West. The gateway to the West, the Prairie Provinces of Manitoba, Saskatchewan and Alberta were for years just that, a gateway to a Promised Land beyond. At first the Plains attracted buffalo hunters who were followed by farmers and miners, all of whom eked out a living the hard way through winters with temperatures that go down well below zero and stay there and summers with temperatures above 90 a lot of the time. Mostly, folks just passed through on their way to the mountains beyond, saying "no, thank you!" to houses made of hunks of sod and not a tree in sight to provide fuel for winter fires.

The main route from East to West in Canada passed through a trading post at the junction of the Red and Assiniboine Rivers. The Cree Indians had called the spot "win-nipiy" because of the murky water. The White Man called it Winnipeg, and it's where more than half of all Manitobans live today. Until the railroad reached there in 1886, settlers arrived in Winnipeg by steamboat lured by Government promotions offering the Last of The Best West in the three Prairie Provinces. A lot of them kept going west, but a lot stayed, too, and made Winnipeg their home. By 1870, when Manitoba became part of the Confederation, there were already 12,000 people there and the railroad brought thousands more, including the people who helped build it. The result is a sophisticated city that's home to one of the world's great ballet companies as well as a famous symphony orchestra and a resident opera company.

Out on the farms the dream many young people dream is to live in the city. And the city they dream of is Winnipeg.

There's another dream that's shared by a lot of prairie farm kids. Its name is hockey.

Ice skating wasn't invented in Canada, but anyone would agree it became a fine art there. The old French trappers were probably the first to use ice skates in Canada. It was a terrific way to get around in a place where there were so many rivers and streams that were frozen over for so long. According to legend, the Indians adapted the idea for themselves and found a whole new means of winter mobility, and then the English turned it all into a sport. Or at least that's one version of the story.

Hockey is one of the oldest sports known to man. It evolved into polo in ancient Persia and eventually reached Ireland long before Saint Patrick did. It became Ireland's national sport. They called it hurling. The great Irish hero Cuchulain was said to have carried a ball nine miles on his hurling stick without letting it touch the ground. Someone must have done even better because the sport was carried over to England where they picked up an old French word describing the crooked stick that was key to the game and called it hockey.

Through all those centuries nobody thought of playing the game on ice. And in the less than 200 years since someone did, no one remembers whose idea it was. They do remember it happened in Canada, though, and everyone agrees it happened in the mid-19th century. It was popular enough by 1879 for McGill University to publish uniform rules for the game. And by 1893 enough people were crazy enough about hockey to prompt the Governor General, Lord Stanley of Preston, to invest $50 in a trophy for the amateur champions of Canada. The Stanley Cup today is the symbol of supremacy in the National Hockey League. And the NHL is the symbol that lures so many young people away from the farms on the Canadian prairie.

Kids as young as 14 leave home to make a name for themselves at midget hockey and if they succeed by the time they're 17, and only about one in 100 makes it, they go on tour with a team in the junior leagues where they hope to impress a scout from the major leagues and become one of the one percent who makes the big time.

The stakes are big. To be a pro hockey player means fame and riches far beyond a farm boy's wildest dreams. And the dream is attainable. The very best hockey players in the world come from Canada and many of them come from the country's heartland. But getting there doesn't seem like any fun at all. Distances between towns with worthwhile amateur teams mean that players usually drop out of school because they're away from home too much. As they move up, they can be traded to a different team and wind up thousands of miles from home boarding with a family who may well have given up one of its sons to the same dream.

They don't become eligible for the big league draft before they turn 20 and by that time they're well-seasoned players. In fact, NHL play may turn out to be easier. One young player, who said, "if I was working any other job, I'd be just anybody. To be honest, this way, I'm somebody," explained the difference:

"A lot of times in the pro rinks a guy gets thrown into the boards and it sounds like he's getting killed. But those boards give a lot. Here in Manitoba it's concrete halfway up the boards and they don't give at all."

It's not exactly a Huck Finn boyhood, and it isn't really typical of the life of young people on Canadian farms, but it's a route hundreds take for a shot at a better life than they think their fathers had. For every one of them there are hundreds more who wouldn't trade the independence and feeling of freedom of the prairies for the so-called joys of city life. And, in general, those who stay can usually look forward to a better life than their fathers had. And some of them are well-aware that there may be more riches in the ground around home than on any hockey rink anywhere.

The oil and gas boom in Alberta is only part of the prairie future. There's gold and uranium and lead there, too, not to mention other resources no one has found yet. There are huge areas no one has explored, which, all by itself is a good reason why a great many young people wouldn't consider leaving and why so many people from other places have been picking up stakes and moving there.

In spite of all the new ways to make a living, the biggest is still farming in what may be the richest wheat fields in the entire world. The black dirt, usually about a foot deep, was the bed of an ocean eons past, and a century ago supported the grass that supported the buffalo. The first white plainsmen were the big buffalo hunters who left a "Western" flair behind them, but a different type followed them. There are more Ukrainians in Manitoba than anywhere else on the American Continent, and they feel right at home there because the countryside is so much like the place their grandfathers left behind. And there may well be more German Mennonites in the Winnipeg area than in all of Pennsylvania, and they've been in Canada almost as long.

What they have the most of in the Prairie Provinces is wide open spaces, punctuated by small towns with wonderful names. The original settlers in the East generally adapted Indian names for their communities, or brought place names with them from Europe. When they went west, they weren't so homesick for the Old Country and they didn't find too many Indian-named landmarks where they wanted to establish their towns. So they were more inventive. Sometimes they kept the names the French trappers had brought for places like Portage la Prairie and Dauphin and Flin Flon in Manitoba. Sometimes cooler heads prevailed and the first settlers' names for places were changed by later arrivals, as was the case for Pile of Bones, Saskatchewan, which was renamed Regina in honor of Queen Victoria just before the Mounties arrived to make it their headquarters.

But people mailing postcards back home often make it a point to make sure they are postmarked in places like

Medicine Hat or Bickerdike, Alberta; or Wartime, Choiceland or Eyebrow, Saskatchewan; or Overflowing River, Windygates or Sundown, Manitoba.

The Bloodvein River flows through part of Manitoba and people from Moose Jaw, Saskatchewan, often run down to Old Wives Lake for a change of scene. Futher west, the Oldman River flows down out of the mountains in the general direction of Manyberries and Seven Persons, Alberta.

High River, Alberta is along the line that separates the prairies from the Rocky Mountains, but the place most people go for their first look at the Rockies gets its name, via one of the Mounties who established a post there, from a bay in Scotland called Calgary.

Calgary has led an almost charmed life since the railroad arrived there in 1883. A lot of people on their way west took a look at the mountains beyond and decided to go no further. A lot of cattle ranchers from the American Plains moved their herds north where the grass was greener and decided to make Calgary their home base. Even before World War I they were pumping oil from the ground nearby and in the years since bigger and better oil fields have been found.

But even if the wildcatters had come up dry, Calgary would still be a place to reckon with, thanks to Guy Weadick, a professional cowboy who wandered into town in 1912. Guy had done a good bit of traveling all over the world with Buffalo Bill's Wild West Show but he had a hankering to settle down and Calgary was the place he picked.

Like most of Buffalo Bill's proteges, he found settling down next to impossible. Instead of looking for a job with local ranchers, he went to them with a unique proposition. If they would stake him, he'd head back south to round up the meanest horses, the stubbornest bulls, the wildest cowboys and even some Red Indians for added spice. He'd bring them back, he said, and put on the wildest Wild West Show ever produced. They liked the idea and sent him on his way, his pockets jingling with their money.

He wasn't gone long, and when he came back he had the seeds of a tradition with him. He called it the Calgary Stampede. Beginning every year in the first or second week of July, the 10-day Stampede is much more than just a tradition, it's the most famous rodeo in the world, featuring the best bronco riders, steer wrestlers, trick ropers and bull riders from all over the United States and Canada.

Naturally, the New West is as much a part of the Stampede as the Old, and today the celebration includes a carnival midway and Las Vegas-style entertainment and gambling. But the profit motive doesn't get in the way of the fun. And, as they say, it comes but once a year. The pace of the city is fast all year, but it's a surprisingly comfortable place.

Even today, Calgary can be called a "boom town," and one of the things that keeps it that way is a strong desire to stay one step (or more!) ahead of its neighbor to the north, the capital of Alberta, Edmonton.

Edmonton became big enough to be called a city during the Gold Rush into the Yukon at the beginning of the 20th century. A lot of prospectors never found gold in "them thar hills," but practically everybody in Edmonton profited from their city's location as the place to stock up for the long trip into the wilderness. It was a good rehearsal for the oil boom that would hit Alberta 50 years later.

Every summer, just about the same time as the Calgary cowboys are packing up their gear for another year, Edmonton celebrates its past with a two-week binge they call "Klondike Days." No matter that the Klondike River is far, far away in the Yukon, it's a good excuse for a good time and everybody in town takes advantage of it. Most people go around town in turn-of-the-century costumes and, in fact, conduct citizen's arrests on people who don't. Some people have been known to spend the entire two weeks looking for gold at the bottom of a beer stein.

It's inevitable that Calgary and Edmonton compete with each other for attention during the month of July. But, fortunately for people objective enough to think both the Stampede and Klondike Days are terrific fun, they don't overlap and it's possible to enjoy both if you have the stamina.

Both cities would be Meccas for tourists even without any razzle-dazzle. They sit on the edge of the Rocky Mountains within easy distance of Banff and Jasper National Parks.

Together the Parks cover 200 square miles of the most beautiful mountain scenery anywhere in the world. Banff is the older, in terms of its life as a park, and is more developed than Jasper. But the resorts, craft shops and hotels clustered around the town of Banff don't intrude on the wonders that nature put there. It became a tourist center when the Canadian Pacific built a hotel there to lure people to the natural sulphur springs. But "taking the waters" has never been as popular with North Americans as it is with Europeans, and though there is a hot springs pool at Banff, it's far from being the area's most popular attraction. It doesn't attract as many people as the cablecars that go to the tops of two of the mountain peaks or rafting on the Bow River or taking long walks on quiet mountain trails.

Lake Louise is part of the Park, the best part probably. There are hundreds of lakes in this part of the Rockies, and all of them are beautiful, but the setting of Lake Louise, with high mountain peaks all around and the Victoria Glacier behind it, makes it something very special indeed.

People who can't get enough of mountain scenery often head north from Colorado by way of Wyoming and Montana and into Canada through Glacier National Park. Even the most unbiased American travelers say that Glacier gets the prize for being the most beautiful of all of the continent's National Parks. But, interestingly, the Rockies get more beautiful as they stretch north. The majority of the highest peaks in the range are in Canada and the lion's share of them are in Banff National Park. Lake Louise itself, at 5,051 feet, is the highest town in Canada and there are a dozen mountains within easy distance of it that are twice as high.

There are glaciers in the park, too, some as thick as a skyscraper is high. But Jasper is the place for exploring them. The Columbia Ice Fields cover more than 160 square miles of Jasper National Park with a sheet of ice that is often as much as a thousand feet thick. Visitors go out onto the glacier in giant snowmobiles and often spend the night at a hotel that's been built on top of the ice.

The Continental Divide runs down the spine of the Rockies through Alberta. Today it's one of nature's wonders that still impresses people, but with a different kind of awe than impressed our grandfathers. Until a little more than a generation ago, the mountains were a wall that separated British Columbia from the rest of Canada. The railroads, highways and the airplane have changed that somewhat, but there's still a wall there, even if it's only psychological.

Vancouver is Canada's most important seaport, but a sailor who puts in there will find it quite different from ports he's visited in the East. Its climate is rainy and foggy and in winter it's not like the common impression of Canada at all. Its mid-30s average, in fact, is downright tropical compared even to other parts of British Columbia. It's cooler in summer than the Canadian average, too.

The people are more like Americans than other Canadians, but like other Canadians they don't find the comparison at all flattering. As in the Western United States, the conversation over business lunches often turns to the trials and tribulations of doing business with "The East." But when the talk is overheard at Vancouver's Le Pavillon, the term "East" more often means Japan or New Zealand than Montreal or Toronto. Vancouver is 350 miles closer to Tokyo than it is to Halifax, on Canada's East Coast, and markets are growing faster in the Far East anyway, which makes British Columbia's future brighter than ever.

It's always been a place to look for a good future. The 18th-century explorers knew it, and the fur trappers who followed them were sure of it. The cattlemen who drove their longhorns there from the American ranges never regretted not going back. But the search for a bright future has never been approached as enthusiastically as it was in the 1860s, during the Cariboo Gold Rush.

It all started in 1862, when a prospector named Billy Barker dug a hole and came up with $5 million worth of gold nuggets. Within a few months a town grew around the hole, called Barkerville, of course, and thousands of miners went to work trying to duplicate the feat. By 1865, the population had grown to some 10,000, making it far and away the biggest town in the Canadian West.

A lot of the people did get rich and a lot of those who did never dug an ounce of gold from the ground. At night, when it was too dark to poke around the creek beds, the prospectors generally went into town for a little entertainment. They found plenty of it in saloons and dance halls where there were girls who would gladly smile at a tired miner in exchange for a glass of French champagne and a generous tip. There were friendly games of cribbage to while away the evening hours, too, and friendly people willing to make it more interesting with small wagers.

The restaurants were high-priced, and rarely memorable for quality. But business was good no matter what the business, and stores and banks and offices sprouted up anywhere there was room and by the time the town had stopped growing there was only one open street left, the others having been filled in by buildings.

But if it was crowded, who cared? People were making thousands of dollars a day, and that made it all worthwhile. As one of them wrote in a letter back home (which, significantly, didn't have any money enclosed), "Times good, grub high, whiskey bad, money plenty."

The man who started it all, poor old Billy Barker, took up with a dance hall girl who took him for all he had.

Barkerville itself nearly came to a sad end over a dance hall girl, too. One afternoon in 1868 a miner looked into the back door of a saloon and saw one of the girls ironing her petticoat. Smitten, he leaned through the doorway and tried to kiss her. But in the process he knocked over a stove and set fire to the place. The whole town was made of canvas and dry wood and it didn't take long for the fire to destroy the saloon and spread to the bank next door.

In 20 minutes the whole town was on fire and an hour later, 15 saloons, two banks, the newspaper office, a church, eight boarding houses and three breweries were reduced to ashes along with some 100 other buildings. Only one life was lost, but most of the people of Barkerville had nothing left but the clothes on their backs. But they still had their knack for making money and some of them got very rich rebuilding the town; a project that began the very next day.

The price of lumber doubled overnight, but so did the cost of labor and within weeks the town was rebuilt and thriving. Everybody was making money from everybody else and there was still enough gold under their feet to make it all worthwhile.

Eventually the gold was gone and the "new" Barkerville became a ghost town. But the ghosts are still interesting to anyone who visits the town. And who knows? A tourist panning for gold in Williams Creek might get lucky and start the whole thing all over again.

There's a frontier spirit in British Columbia. It's cowboy country, including one ranch that's bigger than the King Ranch in Texas and another that's bigger than the State of Rhode Island. The Pacific coastline with all its inlets would stretch out to 7,000 miles, which is why so many people make their living by fishing. The Province is almost completely covered by mountains, and about three-quarters of it is covered by thick forests. But it's cosmopolitan, too. When Queen Elizabeth arrived in Vancouver over a dozen years ago, her daughter, Princess Anne, said: "Mother, this is just like home."

It's not, of course. She may have had the weather in mind. But as a city Vancouver doesn't take a back seat to any place, not even London. A century ago there wasn't much there but a sawmill and a couple of saloons. By 1886 it had grown enough to be officially called a city, and ten years later the railroad broke through and it became a city with a future.

It was inevitable there would be a city on the spot. The natural harbor, with close to 100 miles of waterfront, is one of the best in the world. The mountains around it make it a beautiful setting, too. And when the sun shines (yes, of course the sun shines on Vancouver), it's like paradise itself. When the sun comes out, so do the natives, intent on soaking up every drop of it on a boat, on a mountainside or in Stanley Park, easily the most beautiful urban park in Canada, possibly in the whole world.

It's a well-designed 1,000-acre wilderness preserve inside the city, but surrounded on three sides by the sea. Some of the park has been landscaped into formal gardens, but the evergreen forests with marked trails provide a feeling of peace and quiet few other city parks offer. It's a great place for hiking, for jogging, for listening to a concert or riding a bike. It's a terrific place for a picnic, and the city thoughtfully provides hot water for people who like a spot of tea with their picnic sandwiches.

It's possible to walk about seven miles along the seawall, and if a dip in the ocean seems like a good idea after that, there are beaches, too, and the water is warmer than Vancouver's northern latitude might suggest. Beyond it, the English Bay area looks a good bit like Rio, but without the sweltering sun.

The main influence in Vancouver is Scottish, but like most important cities, it's a multi-national place with French and Americans everywhere as well as other Europeans and a growing number of Japanese. It also has the biggest Chinatown of any city in North America except San Francisco.

Vancouverites have been called the luckiest of Canadians because they're privileged to live in such a beautiful place. It's a feeling visitors get the minute they leave the airport. In most of the world's cities, the trip from the airport to downtown is, to be polite, uninspiring. But not in Vancouver. Here it can be called a joy ride and no one could deny it. In Vancouver it's only the beginning. It's a city that keeps getting better.

Visitors to Vancouver are twice-blessed because less than two hours away by boat is Vancouver Island, the biggest of the Pacific Coast islands, stretching about 300 miles northward from the United States-Canada border.

The Southern part of the Island, around Victoria, is where most of the people live, and many of those people are retired Britons who have migrated here to surroundings that remind them of home, but with a climate they find agreeable the year 'round. The result is that Victoria has wrapped itself in British tradition. Tours of the city are conducted in double-decked buses, the shops sell English tweeds and bone china and many of the buildings are patterned after English cottages and castles. Some of the buildings, including the Parliament Buildings, are even Victorian. But Victoria is not England, and though it's a charming place, it's not all there is to Vancouver Island, either.

One of the nice things about Victoria is the beautiful mountain range that forms a background to it. The mountains reach a height of more than 7,000 feet at Mount Golden Hind and, along the shore, they create dramatic fjords and rocky cliffs.

According to an old Indian legend, this is the place where the world began and everything else is only a reflection of it. Fortunately, very little has been done to improve on the Great Spirit's work, and the land on most of Vancouver Island is not much different than it was when the first Indians found it a perfect place to live.

Before then, the legend goes, there was nothing in the world but water. There was no earth, no trees or flowers and no animals. The Great Spirit needed companionship so he created the otter, the beaver and the muskrat. But there was no land for them to walk on.

He asked the muskrat to dive down to the bottom of the sea and bring back some earth. The muskrat did as he was asked, but after long hours came back empty-handed. He was too tired to try again and so the beaver tried. The Great Spirit had promised each of them fish to eat if they succeeded, but after days of searching for the bottom of the sea, neither of them was able to come back with dirt in his paws.

Then the Great Spirit asked the otter to try and promised him a wife to share the land with him if he could succeed. It took a long, long time, but finally the otter came back with the needed earth. The Great Spirit took it and made more from it, which he used to build a beautiful land surrounded by water. Then he kept his promise and made a wife for the otter. When he saw how happy this made the otter, he made other animals, too, always careful to make a wife for each of them. Then he made the Indian people and there was room for all of them to live in peace in the wonderful land that would one day be called Vancouver Island.

The otter is still probably the happiest of all animals, and Vancouver Island is a great place to watch them play. It's also a wonderful place for deer and eagles, bear and elk, cougar and, of course, beavers and muskrats.

Sea-lions and seals sun themselves on the Island's rocks and whales swim in the waters around it. And the Indian people have left their mark there in the form of incredible totem poles. They've left their descendants there, too, and the Indians are just as friendly today as their ancestors were in 1778, when Captain Cook put ashore at their village of Yuquot on the Pacific side and renamed it Friendly Cove.

British Columbia was the last of what we call the Western World to become a part of it. And, though they are growing fast, many parts of the Province are exactly the same today as they were when the Hudson's Bay people began establishing forts all over the place. Logging companies have cut trees, mining companies have dug holes and they've established little towns for the people who work for them. But the landscape is still wild and woolly, and it gets wilder and woollier as it goes north.

British Columbia borders on four American states: Montana, Idaho and Washington on the south and Alaska on the northwest. But due north is a place of legend, an adventure called Yukon.

Writing in *The New York Times*, Andy Malcolm, of The Times Toronto Bureau offered this capsule description of the Yukon Territory:

"Ordinary travelers seeking ordinary vacations should not go to the Yukon. It is not reachable by ordinary Interstate highways. There are no ordinary amusement parks, no ordinary tall towers with ordinary revolving restaurants and no ordinary sumptuous hotels with ordinary Olympic-size swimming pools. Ordinary tourist attractions are few and far – very far – between. Ordinary food is hard to come by; there is not even a McDonald's in the whole territory.

"What the Yukon Territory does have for North American vacationers is, well, extraordinary. And beautiful. And historic. And dangerous at times. It has few people. It has many wild animals. It has space. So much space that the Royal Canadian Mounted Police, who provide local police protection, spend far more time searching for lost people than writing parking tickets. And the air is so clean you cannot even see it.

"It has mountainsides so expansive they dwarf the shadows of clouds drifting overhead. It has winds so strong they roll up snowballs the size of a human head. It has trails that could easily lead a lone traveler to his death – though it would surely be a scenic one. It has winter nights, and summer days, that never end."

On a trip through the Yukon a while back, Andy stopped for gas and some sourdough pancakes at a little place called Moose Creek. As they were driving away, his son asked him why an American flag was flying over the cabin. As a reporter, he knew the best way to find out was to ask, and in the process he met a pair of fellow New Yorkers whose reason for being in the Yukon Territory is typical of many of the 23,000 people who make no attempt to look like a crowd in an area about the size of Texas.

The owners told him they had been on their way back from a trip to Alaska when their car broke down near Moose Creek, which is not a town at all but a combination tea room and gas station about 50 miles from the nearest "civilization." They worked off the cost of repairs and lodging by working the hand-operated gas pump and cutting wood and then went on their way. But they couldn't get Moose Creek out their system, and less than a year later they were back with a proposition to buy the place. Their offer was accepted and now they're in business. He runs the gas station and cuts the wood (it takes more than 23 cords to make it through a winter) and helps her with the restaurant kitchen. They're busy in the summer, but things slow down quite a bit when the temperature goes down and the nights get long. "We just put on a pot of soup all day and relax." It's not New York, to be sure, "but there's plenty of bustle right here," they say. "The Yukon is a land of opportunity the way the United States used to be."

They have a better word for opportunity in the Yukon. It's an old Spanish word that sailors used to describe fair weather. In the Yukon it became another word for prosperity when they renamed Rabbit Creek Bonanza. And what a bonanza they found there!

The Hudson's Bay Company, who established trading posts in the Yukon in the 1850s, knew there was gold there but did all they could to discourage prospecting. They had a plan for the area's economy and it was based on furs. But it's hard to keep a good idea down and, by 1886, some miners were making as much as $100 a day along the Stewart River. If it doesn't sound like much, consider the fact that a Hudson's Bay trader earned about $300 a year back then.

But then as now, it was rough country and not more than a hundred or so hardy men were willing to endure a Yukon winter. The boom began when Bob Henderson arrived in the Territory from Nova Scotia. He found some promising prospects along the lower Yukon River and when he met a fishing party on his way south, he told them about it.

It was customary in those days to share the wealth and Henderson recommended that the fishermen go have a look at the gravel in Rabbit Creek. The head of the party was George Washington Carmak, a prospector who had married a Siwash Indian girl and in the process had become an outcast among the other whites in the area, who called him "Siwash George." With him was his wife and her two brothers, Snookum Jim and Tagish Charlie. They decided to go have a look and promised Henderson they'd send back word if they found anything interesting.

By the time they reached Rabbit Creek their supplies were low and Snookum Jim went on ahead to do some hunting. When he stopped for a drink in the creek, he noticed something shiny at the bottom. It was gold, of course, and quickly the three men staked out claims.

Forgetting all about Henderson, Charlie and George headed for Fortymile to register their claims and do a little boasting. But when they got there, nobody believed their story. Rabbit Creek ran through a wide valley, too wide for gold to be there. Besides, who'd take the word of an Indian-lover? Rabbit Creek was a good moose pasture, they all said, but a terrible spot for a gold field. And with that, they turned back to the bar to order another round. But the bartender wasn't there. **He** believed George and was on his way north to stake a claim. He eventually became half-owner of a mine, which earned him $130,000 in the first year and he personally pulled a one-pound nugget of pure gold from the ground. He never tended bar again.

It wasn't long before the creek was completely staked-out and the gold rush was on. But poor Bob Henderson wasn't in on it. He had gone south and by the time word reached him, there were no claims left. He went back to Nova Scotia very poor and very bitter, and though the Canadian Government officially recognized him as the discoverer of the Klondike and offered him a pension, he told them he didn't want their money and went to British Columbia in 1927 to find another Bonanza. He never did.

Snookum Jim and Taglish Charlie were made honorary Canadian citizens for their part in the find, a very special status for Indians in those days. Siwash George, who was an American citizen, left his family and drifted to New York, where he died broke.

But the pay-dirt they found in that old moose pasture made a lot of people very rich. In the first four years their strike produced more than $30 million worth of gold and by 1906, when the area was considered "worked out," the official value of the gold taken from the Klondike was about $200 million. And that's not counting the countless prospectors who quietly worked their claims and quietly went away without telling anyone how much gold they had.

In the days of the big strikes, Dawson became one of the

biggest cities in Canada, with a population of some 30,000. Today, with 700, it's officially the smallest city in the country. And a lot of its citizens are there hoping to strike it rich again. The lure is still as strong as it was back when Robert Service wrote, "It grips you like some kinds of sinning."

Yukoners are a friendly bunch and they love a good party. In Dawson City they celebrate spring twice, at the end of March and again in the middle of May. They celebrate the discovery of gold with a week-long festival and they even have an "International Outhouse Race" in September. They have similar festivities at Faro and Whitehorse, too, always punctuated with hard-drinking, wild dancing and a general Gay 90s atmosphere. But it's not easy to think of "sinning" on a tour of the Yukon. The vastness of the landscape, the incredible beauty of its unspoiled wilderness inspires thoughts of how sinful it is there aren't more places in the world like this.

There simply isn't another place in the world like Canada. And some day Canadians might even agree on what makes it such a wonderful place. For now, though, there is, as they may say, a difference of opinion.

For most of its history, Canada had a flag that was based on the British Union Jack. Naturally, the French-speaking citizens found it hard to be respectful of it and a debate raged for years before they compromised and adoped a red maple leaf as the official standard in 1965.

But that debate was puny compared to the controversy that preceded the introduction of "O Canada" as the official national anthem in 1980. It was the unofficial musical symbol of Canada for a century before that, but even now there are citizens who think it was a terrible choice.

In the first place, it's a French song. It was written in 1880 by a Quebec musician and, with words by a Montreal judge, was always sung at festivities marking St.Jean-Baptiste Day, the "national" holiday of Quebec. In 1908, an English-speaking Canadian wrote new words that are more-or-less the official words today, but he probably wouldn't recognize his work.

Disputes from every part of the country have resulted in changing nearly all the words except his first four lines:

> "O Canada! Our home and native land,
> True patriot love in all thy sons command.
> With glowing hearts we see thee rise,
> The true North strong and free!"

But even those lines are the subject of bitter protest. "What do you mean 'native land?'" asked the sons of immigrants. "What do you mean 'sons'?" shouted the feminists, who began letter-writing campaigns to get "sexist" words out of the national anthem. Then the left-over flower children, who don't think much of national anthems anyway, protested about putting the words "love" and "patriot" next to each other. And Westerners complained about the reference to the "true North," but Easterners stand firmly against changing it. Even atheists have complained because the anthem mentions God. And they get into a peculiar kind of conflict with Canadians who propose scrapping the whole thing in favor of "God Save the Queen."

That would never do, of course; there are a great many Canadians who don't care if He does or not. And that, more than anything else, is why the Government decided to go to all the trouble to give them an anthem of their own. In the process they proved it isn't easy to be a politician in Canada. Or a poet.

It took 17 years to get a law on the books that made "O Canada" official. Then, when the lawmakers stepped out onto the lawn in front of Ottawa's Parliament Building to sing it for the first time, a new problem came up. Should they sing it in French or in English? But Canadian politicians know how to handle a problem like that. They sang it in both languages simultaneously after dividing the group of singers in half (very carefully, of course). It probably would have worked very well if everyone had remembered the words. At least they were singing together, which is something that doesn't always happen in Canada.

The search for a "typical" Canadian or a representative Canadian experience would drive the most patient researcher crazy. There simply isn't any such thing. It's a country with vast outdoor opportunities, and hundreds of national parks coupled with a network of provincial parks (British Columbia alone has 120 of them!) would make it seem to be a land of hunters, campers and fishermen. Yet it has more enclosed shopping malls, both underground and above, per capita than any other country in the world. As a country, it has never been subjected to a major invasion, yet it has more restored forts than most other countries. In the midst of natural splendor it has more than its share of wax museums and amusement parks.

The biggest industrial giant in Canada is General Motors, based in Detroit, Michigan, U.S.A. And many famous Canadians have gone to the United States to make their mark, including James Naismith, who invented the game of basketball in Boston and Mack Sennett who exported the Keystone Kops from Hollywood. Louis B. Meyer went to Hollywood from Canada, too, and Lord Thompson of Fleet built a British newspaper empire from Canada. Canadian musicians run the gamut from jazz pianist Oscar Peterson to arranger Percy Faith to pop star Gordon Lightfoot and opera singer Jon Vickers. Saul Bellow, the author, is Canadian, so is Will Durant. Raymond Massey, the actor, came from Canada, so did William Shattner and so did Margot Kidder.

But if there's been a talent drain in the past, the day seems to be at hand when young people will be content to make their mark at home in Canada. It's already happening in music and dance as well as in the other arts. And there's a new nationalism that unites most Canadians in spite of all the things that divide them. They look southward and they see the "American Dream" stalled in a sea of commercialism. They read the words of their countryman, the late Marshall McLuhan who put his finger on some of the problems of America's media-oriented society, and they look around and they say "Hey, look at us! We have all the things they said they wanted and we don't have the problems. Time is on our side."

The future is very much on their side. Pierre Trudeau put his finger on it when he said: "Canadians are discovering for the first time that this country is a fabulous place."

And one of the things that makes it fabulous is a wonderful feeling of diversity in a world that seems bent on sameness.

Inflatable craft in Second Canyon on the Nahanni River.

This page: a trip on the Nahanni River. Right: Rafferty's Riffle, (bottom right) Virginia Falls and (bottom left) a Sea Otter plane lands supplies. Facing page: a bear fishing in the Nell River.

Yellowknife is the largest city in the Territories and is set on a beautiful site on the northern shore of the Great Slave Lake. The city has both a New Town (previous pages, above and overleaf, right) and an Old Town (facing page). Overleaf, left: the Indian settlement on nearby Latham Island.

55

Previous pages: Yellowknife with (left) Yellowknife Bay in the distance. During the long, cold months of winter the Ice Road across the frozen Yellowknife Bay between Detah and Yellowknife comes into operation (these pages and overleaf).

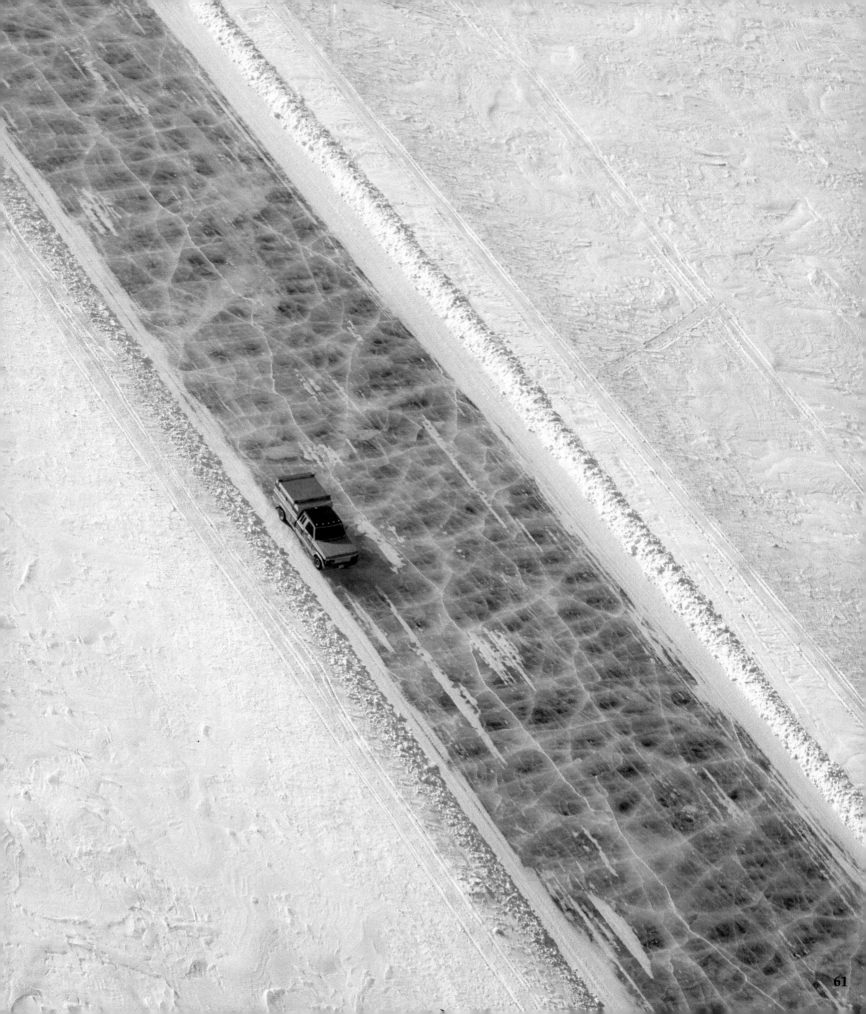

These pages: the modern face of the Northwest Territories shows the Giant Yellowknife Mines workings (above) and motorised transport at Detah (facing page). Overleaf: the more traditional forms of transport in the snowbound land.

YUKON

The Alaska Highway (above) runs across a plateau from which it is impossible to see Whitehorse, barely half a mile to the east. Whitehorse (overleaf), with its historic sternwheeler SS Klondike (facing page), owes its fortune to the railway which was pushed inland from Skagway in 1900 to avoid the rapids of Miles Canyon, and now has some 13,000 inhabitants.

Previous pages and overleaf: Whitehorse, capital of the Yukon, includes some 162 square miles in its boundaries and preserves much of the old gold rush days. Above: the road to Atlin. Facing page: Riverdale.

ISAAC O. STRINGER — 'THE BISHOP WHO ATE HIS BOOTS'
A farm boy from Kincardin,Ontario, graduate of University of Toronto
and Wycliffe College, ordained in 1892 for Mackenzie River to serve
among Loucheaux Indians, Eskimo, and American whalers.
    Married Sarah Ann Alexander and ministered at Herschel Island until
    snowblindness forced them to leave, in 1901.
    Came to Whitehorse in 1903, as rector, health improves.
    Elected second Bishop of Diocese in 1905, to succeed the aging
       Bishop W.C. Bompas, 'The Apostle of the North'.
    In 1907 held first Diocesan Synod here:—moves See from
       Fortymile to Dawson City—moves there himself. Serves next
       25 years travelling far and wide as famous 'Bishop of Yukon'
    1931-4 concludes life as Archbishop of Rupert's Land in Winnipeg.

Previous pages: (left) Whithorse from the south and (right) the Old Log Church, built in 1900. Above: a ski-plane and (facing page) snowbound scenes in and around Atlin. Overleaf: (left) the Yukon River in Miles Canyon and (right) the suburbs of Whitehorse.

These pages and overleaf: hardy climbers brave the rigours of Mount Logan in Kluane National Park. The park is massive and contains some of Canada's highest peaks and most majestic scenery.

Facing page: Lions Gate Bridge links Vancouver with West Vancouver. Above: Vancouver city centre from the Harbour Centre. Overleaf: (left) sunset over English Bay and (right) Horseshoe Bay, northwest of Vancouver.

Above and overleaf, left: Horseshoe Bay, where a plaque commemorates Captain George Vancouver. Facing page: yachts lie moored in Coal Harbour. Overleaf, right: evening in Vancouver.

Above: Vancouver's Coal Harbour from the Harbour Centre. Facing page: the moorings of the Royal Vancouver Yacht Club. Overleaf: the Bloedel Conservatory in Vancouver's Queen Elizabeth Park, which exhibits a large number of tropical plants.

In 1862 three Englishmen arrived at Burrard Inlet and opened a brickworks. For this they were dubbed 'the three greenhorns' by other westerners, but their judgement cannot have been too bad for their works grew to become Vancouver (these pages and overleaf).

These pages: the Butchart Gardens, north of Victoria, which were created some eighty years ago out of an ugly lime quarry by Jennie Butchart, wife of the quarry owner. Overleaf: (left) sunset over Burrard Inlet and (right) Horseshoe Bay.

104

Above: the Gastown area of Vancouver is now the city's chic neighbourhood, with boutiques and fashionable shops, though it started life last century as a drinking quarter for sawmill workers. Facing page: dusk in downtown Vancouver. Overleaf: two views of the False Creek Marina.

Above: driftwood on the rocks of Pacific Rim National Park's South Beach and (facing page) the dense forest of one of the park's islands. Overleaf: (left) an Indian totem pole at the Victoria Heritage Court Complex and (right) the Princess Patricia in Coal Harbour.

North of Vancouver lies Squamish, on the Howe Sound, and further north still is the popular ski resort of Mount Whistler. Between the two stretch the snow-covered Rockies (these pages and overleaf).

Above: snow-clad mountains near Squamish. Facing page: blossoming orchards in the Okanagan Valley. Overleaf: (left) the township of Field, in the heart of Yoho National Park, and (right) Mount Robson, which lies further to the north.

Previous pages: (left) the Robson River and Mount Robson in Mount Robson Provincial Park and (right) a mountain lake. These pages: Whistler Mountain hosts the Molson World Downhill Championships. On the day of the contest competitors ski down the hill carrying their nations' flags. Overleaf: nearby mountain scenes.

Previous pages: smooth snow and jagged peaks near Squamish. Above: the excitement of the Prince George Professional Rodeo. Facing page: Main Street, in the restored gold rush town of Barkerville. Overleaf: (left) the CN Railway crossing the North Thompson River and (right) Pavilion Lake near Lillooet.

SALOON

JOE DENNY, Proprietor.

Previous pages: (left) a train entering the spiral tunnel under Mount Ogden by Kicking Horse Pass, whose purpose is explained on a board (right). Above: Fort Steele Historic Park, a reconstructed Kootenay fort and town of the 1890-1905 era. Facing page: a tractor in the Okanagan Valley. Overleaf: the Rockies near Squamish.

Previous pages: (left) a mountain near Squamish and (right) Mount Whistler Ski Resort. Victoria is the capital of British Columbia and contains the Parliament Buildings (above and overleaf, right) and the Empress Hotel (facing page). Overleaf, left: the calm waters of Lillooet Lake.

Facing page: the Legislative Building in Edmonton, which was opened in 1912. Above and overleaf: the Muttart Conservatory, whose glass pyramids contain flora from three different climatic regions.

50

6

7

Above: the ice rink in the West Edmonton Mall. Facing page: the Muttart Conservatory and Edmonton skyline. Overleaf: (left) central Edmonton and (right) Calgary's Family of Man sculpture by Mario Armengol.

The thrusting skyline of Calgary (these pages) includes the 600-foot-tall, red and white Calgary Tower which features a restaurant and observation deck. Overleaf: the excitement of the Calgary Stampede.

Above: Medicine Lake, which for much of the year is little more than a dry gravel bed, until filled by spring's melting snows. Facing page: the silky waters of Peyto Lake, in the heart of Banff National Park. Overleaf: the rich farmlands of the Albertan prairies.

Previous pages: two views of the Athabasca River. Above: hoodoos in Dinosaur Valley, near Drumheller. Facing page: Writing-on-Stone Provincial Park. Overleaf: spring and winter scenes at Moraine Lake in the Valley of the Ten Peaks, Banff National Park.

Above: the Sunshine Ski Resort. Facing page: the frozen banks of the Athabasca River in Jasper National Park. Overleaf: (left) Mount Eisenhower and the Bow River near Lake Louise, and (right) the modern Highway 93 passing through the Sunwapta Pass.

Previous pages: (left) the pyramidal peak of Mount Assiniboine and (right) the mountain slopes near Banff. Above: a bench on a cleared patch of ice on Lake Louise. Facing page: the Chateau Lake Louise hotel.

Previous pages: (left) the landscape north of Calgary on the Trans-Canada Highway and (right) a river near Yellowhead Pass. Above: a dog team racing across the frozen surface of Lake Louise. Facing page: the mountains near Banff.

Previous pages: (left) the Columbia Icefields and (right) chairlifts at the Lake Louise ski resort. These pages: in the Rocky Mountains stand two towns which share the names of their National Parks: Jasper (above) and Banff (facing page). Overleaf: (left) the Bow River and (right) the peak above Crowfoot Glacier.

184

SASKATCHEWAN

Regina's neo-Renaissance Legislative Building (above), set in a 2,000 acre park, contrasts in style with the startlingly-modern City Hall (facing page). Overleaf: (left) grain elevators in the wheat belt and (right) one of the province's lakes.

Above: a beaver and its lodge in Prince Albert National Park, where Halkett Lake (overleaf, left) can also be found. Facing page: a Wilson's Phalarope in Grasslands National Park. Overleaf, right: a view from the Cypress Hills in the southwestern corner of the state.

The wide open spaces of Saskatchewan (these pages) and the extensive woodlands (previous pages, left), in the north of the province, boast a wide variety of wildlife: (previous pages, right) a bald eagle, (overleaf, left) a prairie rattlesnake and (overleaf, right) a prairie gartersnake.

MANITOBA

Facing page and overleaf, right: the fine neo-Classical Legislative Buildings in Winnipeg were completed in 1919 and are topped by the famous Golden Boy statue. Above: a camper van beside the clear, blue waters of Two Mile Lake in Duck Mountain Provincial Park. Overleaf, left: the reconstructed Mennonite town of Steinbach.

Above: the gentle, rolling farmland of the province. Facing page:
farm buildings at Steinbach. Overleaf: (left) sunrise near
Churchill and (right) the frozen Churchill River in winter.

The small town of Churchill (previous pages), on the shores of the Hudson Bay, was founded in 1685 as a fur trading post and named in honour of John Churchill, distant relative of the more-recently famous Winston Churchill. These pages and overleaf: icebound Churchill Harbour.

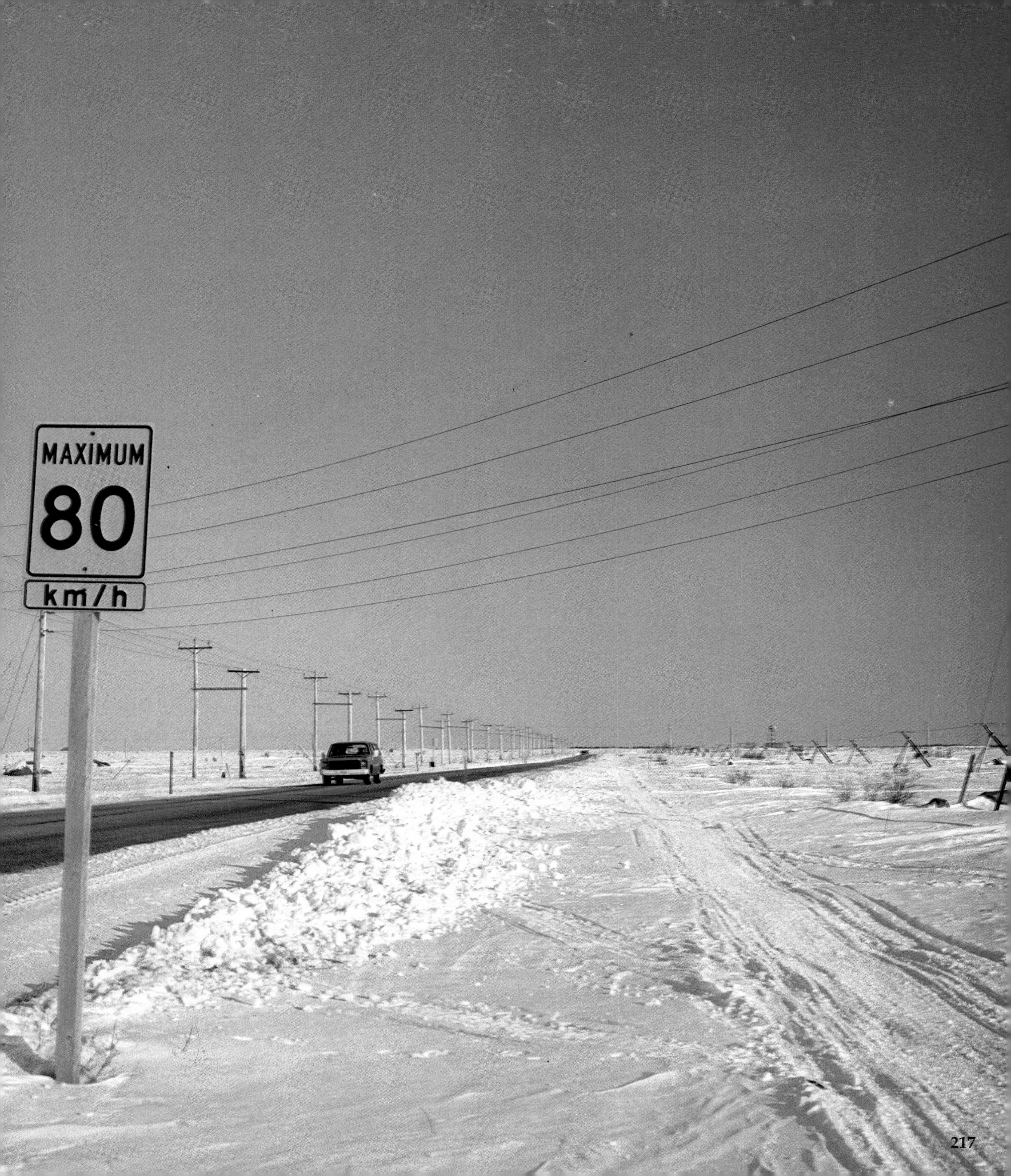
MAXIMUM
80
km/h

Churchill (these and previous pages, overleaf and following pages) is accessible by air from Winnipeg, but its main business is as a railhead serving the vast agricultural hinterland and as a port for the export of grain. Previous pages, left and overleaf, right: a train leaving for Winnipeg. Above and overleaf, left: the station. Facing page: Kelsey Boulevard.

When Port Arthur (above) joined with Fort William in 1970 the new town took its name from the stretch of water on which they both lie: Thunder Bay (facing page), on Lake Superior. Overleaf: (left) the Great Lakes Paper Mill and Mount McKay and (right) the Canadian Ski Jumping Championships, both at Thunder Bay.

Above: sunset over Toronto, seen across the harbour. Facing page: a fine aerial view of the Exhibition Park where the famous 'Ex' is held annually. Overleaf: (left) a ferry plying between the city and Toronto Islands and (right) Ontario Place.

Previous pages: (left) the fine City Hall, built in 1965 to a revolutionary design, and (right) the city in winter. Above: the Ontario Parliament in Queen's Park. Facing page: Nathan Phillips Square. Overleaf: (left) Old City Hall and Nathan Phillips Square and (right) yachts moored at Ontario Place.

Previous pages: (left) the CN Tower and (right) the skyline from the harbour. These pages: the ice canoe race around Toronto Harbour, part of the Molson Winterfest. Overleaf: (left) Casa Loma, a 98-room castle built by Sir Henry Pellatt before the First World War and (right) City Hall and Nathan Phillips Square.

241

Previous pages: the magnificent Eaton Centre, a massive development of shops and offices on Yonge Street. These pages: futuristic Ontario Place, where an exposition is held during the summer. Overleaf: (left) the Royal Bank Plaza and (right and following pages) the city skyline.

Previous pages: (left) splendid architecture at Harbourfront and (right) the Toronto Islands Ferry. Toronto Islands (these pages) offer the citizens a choice of beaches, lagoons and gardens. Overleaf: scenes from the Blue Mountain ski resort.

For some 50-odd miles below Lake Ontario, the St. Lawrence River is littered with islands; an area
known as Thousand Islands (previous pages). Above: one of the province's many rivers. Facing page:
the Jones Falls Locks on the Rideau Canal between Ottawa and Kingston. Overleaf: (left) Kingston
City Hall and (right) the Soo Locks at Sault Ste. Marie.

Previous pages, these pages and overleaf: Niagara Falls. The falls plunge more than 50 metres from the escarpment into the pool below, creating one of the most spectacular sights on the continent.

Almost as much an institution as the capital it serves, the Chateau Laurier (these pages) is one of the finest and most prestigious hotels in the country. Overleaf: the Parliament Buildings in Ottawa and the Rideau Canal.

The Parliament Buildings (previous pages, above and overleaf) in Ottawa were first completed in 1876, but a disastrous fire in 1916 caused the central block to be rebuilt with its lofty Peace Tower. Facing page: an Inuit dog sled at the Winterlude celebrations.

Montreal (these pages and overleaf) is the largest city in Quebec Province, and the second largest French-speaking city in the world. Its huge port facilities and strategic location long ago made this one of Canada's prime industrial and financial centres.

*Northwest of Montreal can be found some of the province's finest ski resorts
including: Gray Rocks Resort (above), Mont Tremblant (facing page and overleaf,
left) and Sainte-Agathe-des-Monts (overleaf, right).*

288

Previous pages: the snow-clad scenery north of Montreal, (left) near St-Jovite and (right) Mont Tremblant Ski Village. The Old City of Quebec includes such buildings as the Chateau Frontenac (above, facing page and overleaf, left), the Holy Trinity Anglican Cathedral (facing page) and the Citadelle (overleaf, right).

QUÉBEC-ALBERTA

QUÉBEC-ALBERTA

QUÉBEC

À LA DÉCOUVERTE DE L'AL

Previous pages, these pages and overleaf: for some ten days in
February Quebec abandons itself to Carnaval, a time of street
parades, snow sculptures and general jollification.

299

The imposing, green-roofed hotel, Le Chateau Frontenac (these pages and previous pages), was built in the style of a 17th-century French chateau and remains an eye-catching landmark to this day. Overleaf: (left) Rue St. Louis decorated for Carnaval and (right) Rue Petit Champlain in the Lower Town.

Previous pages, left: the Pont Pierre Laporte and Pont de Quebec cross the frozen St. Lawrence upstream of the Old City. Above and previous pages, right: a crew participating in a canoe race across the frozen river at Carnaval time. Facing page and overleaf, left: Mont Sainte Anne. Overleaf, right Stoneham Ski Resort.

Previous pages: the ski runs of Mont Sainte Anne, downstream of Quebec City. These pages: scenes from La Mauricie National Park, situated in the Laurentian Highlands, one of the most scenic areas of the province. Overleaf: scenes along the Gaspé Peninsula.

Facing page: Pouch Cove, first settled in 1611. Above and overleaf, left: St. John's, the capital of Newfoundland, dates back to the 16th century and owes its prosperity to the magnificently sheltered harbour. Overleaf, right: Quidi Vidi Village.

Previous pages: (left) the fishing town of Bonavista and (right) an offshore iceberg. Facing page and overleaf, left: typical Newfoundland villages near Twillingate. Above: fishing at Grand Falls. Overleaf, right: Placentia, a French stronghold in the 17th century.

Facing page: Stanhope Cape Lighthouse. Above: North Rustico Harbour on the island's north shore. Overleaf: (left) some of the island's abundant stock and (right) Government House, in Charlottetown, erected in 1834 and home of the province's Lieutenant Governor.

Above: Point Wolfe dam and covered bridge in Fundy National Park. Facing page and overleaf: views of Kings Landing Historical Settlement, a fascinating recreation of village life in the central Saint John River Valley between the years 1790 and 1870.

Previous pages: (left) Kings Landing Historical Settlement and (right) a beach near Saint John. These pages and overleaf, left: Market Square in Saint John, a recently restored area of restaurants, bars and shops in the heart of the city. Overleaf, right: the interior of Fredericton's Officers' Quarters.

344

The staff at Kings Landing Historical Settlement (these pages and overleaf) wear period costume and recreate the rural lifestyle of more than a century ago.

NOVA SCOTIA

Halifax is not only capital of Nova Scotia, but also the financial centre for the Atlantic Provinces. Above and overleaf, right: the city centre. Facing page: the Halifax Public Gardens. Overleaf, left: the Mar II in the Historic Properties area.

From its founding in 1749, Halifax was a military city complete with massive fortifications which today form the star-shaped Citadel (overleaf, left). Above: the 5,239 foot long A. Murray MacKay Bridge. Facing page: the Historic Properties area. Overleaf, right: the waterfront.

The coast of Nova Scotia shelters some of the loveliest communities in the nation. Previous pages, left, facing page and overleaf, right: the coastline near the village of Peggy's Cove (previous pages, right, above, overleaf, left and following pages), perhaps the most idyllic of all the Nova Scotian fishing villages.

Previous pages: (left) Blue Rocks and (right) nearby coastline. Facing page:
Peggy's Cove and (above) another nearby village. Overleaf: (left) boats moored
at Cape St. Mary and (right) Water Street in St. Andrews, on Passamaquoddy Bay.

Previous pages: (left) Clark's Harbour, on the southern tip of Nova Scotia, and (right) the Joe Howe Falls in Truro. Above: driftwood at Halls Harbour. Facing page: the newly restored fortress of Louisbourg, built by the French in 1720 and destroyed by the British in 1760. Overleaf: (left) Glace Bay and (right) the industrial city of Sydney.

*Facing page: a bull elk and (above) a young deer. Overleaf:
(left) buffalo and (right) mountain goat and kid in Jasper
National Park.*

Above: a cinnamon-coloured black bear. Facing page: a mule deer
in the Rockies. Overleaf: (left) a yellow-breasted chat and
(right) a wood duck in Ontario.

Above: a beaver in Kejimkujik National Park. Facing page: a squirrel. Overleaf: (left) a deer with velvet on its antlers and (right) a bull moose, both in Alberta.

Previous pages: (left) a moulting deer and (right) a bighorn sheep. Above: a fawn. Facing page: a bear in the Nell River. Overleaf: (left) Nuttell's cottontail and (right) a ground squirrel. Following page: a barred owl.